Bringing creative teaching into the young learner classroom

Lynne Cameron and Penny McKay

UNIVERSITY PRESS

OXFORD
UNIVERSITY PRESS

Great Clarendon Street, Oxford OX2 6DP

Oxford University Press is a department of the University of Oxford.
It furthers the University's objective of excellence in research, scholarship,
and education by publishing worldwide in

Oxford New York

Auckland Cape Town Dar es Salaam Hong Kong Karachi
Kuala Lumpur Madrid Melbourne Mexico City Nairobi
New Delhi Shanghai Taipei Toronto

With offices in

Argentina Austria Brazil Chile Czech Republic France Greece
Guatemala Hungary Italy Japan Poland Portugal Singapore
South Korea Switzerland Thailand Turkey Ukraine Vietnam

OXFORD and OXFORD ENGLISH are registered trade marks of
Oxford University Press in the UK and in certain other countries

© Oxford University Press 2010

The moral rights of the author have been asserted

Database right Oxford University Press (maker)

First published 2010
2014 2013 2012 2011 2010
10 9 8 7 6 5 4 3 2 1

ISBN: 978 0 19 442248 2

Printed in Spain by Orymu, S.A.

For Penny
whose creativity brightened and inspired many lives

Contents

Introduction

We have written this book because we believe that teachers have a special role to play in a child's language education. Creative teaching, personalized to your learners, can inspire children, create a love of a language, and develop their skills and the confidence that ensure success in language learning.

Who the book is for

You may be a teacher new to working with young children or a teacher with years of experience. English may be your first language or it may be your second, third, or even fourth.

If you are a new teacher, we suggest that you read about the activities to get a feel for the range of possibilities in the young learner classroom and begin with the activities that feel easiest for you. Use a five-minute time slot at the beginning or middle of a lesson to try something new rather than waiting wait until the end of a lesson, when you and the children may be tired or rushed. Afterwards, you might want to record in a teaching journal the children's reactions, their use of English, what they learnt, and how you felt when leading the activity. Your creativity as a teacher will develop through small steps, combined with noticing closely what happens for the children you teach.

If you are an experienced teacher, we hope that the teaching suggestions in the book will give you new ideas to use with your learners. Your creativity as a teacher springs from your experience and knowledge, and we hope our book offers an extra spark to boost your enthusiasm.

The learners

This book is about learners who are children. We have targeted the age range of 5–12 years, although some activities will work with children who are outside of this age range. Both age level and language level need to be taken into account when planning activities for the classroom.

Younger children (aged 5–6) need shorter activities because their attention span is shorter: they will concentrate for five minutes but find a 15-minute task too long. They need to move around more than older learners, and they may still be mastering fine motor skills, like careful colouring in or cutting with scissors, and so need language activities that are not too physically demanding in these ways. Young children work best in pairs or in teacher-led activities. They are intensely curious, and if you can let them ask questions or talk about what they are doing, you will find many opportunities to enhance their learning by following their interests. Learner-led talk will probably be in a mixture of English and first language. Mixing languages does not matter in informal talk but it will help the children if you separate English from home languages in your talk.

Older children (aged 7–12) need activities that are challenging in content even if the English is simple. They may get more frustrated with the demands of learning a new language, and as they get older they may get embarrassed by speaking in English. Children this age can work for longer on activities and can be trained to work productively in groups of four or five. Reading and writing in English becomes easier to include in activities but we urge you to check that children really understand what they read and write, and that print is not just a 'code' without meaning for them.

Don't be afraid to try activities outside of the suggested age range. Younger children may enjoy parts of activities aimed at older children. Older children may enjoy activities aimed at younger children, especially if you tell them that they are testing out activities for children younger than them. This not only gives them a sense of responsibility but also further practice in the language they learnt at earlier stages, which gives them a chance to feel fluent and competent in English.

Using English

In all activities, we have tried to encourage the use of spoken English by teachers. This is for three reasons: (1) because children are naturally equipped to learn from talk, especially at the younger end of the age range, (2) because using written English will limit the participation of some children who find reading and/or writing difficult, and (3) because the English classroom (and the English teacher) may be the children's main source of English language and we don't want to lose a minute of that valuable time.

Some activities include samples of classroom language that teachers can use. We have included these to help teachers in various ways. If you are new to teaching children, you can see what child learners can be expected to understand. If English is not your first language, you can see examples of 'natural' teacher-child talk. If English is your first language, you can see how to simplify English so that children understand and are engaged.

Thanks

We would like to thank the student teachers and the experienced teachers we have worked with over the years for their creativity and inspiration. It is impossible to thank each one of you individually, but we hope that if you find one of your ideas in this book, you will be pleased to share it with the rest of the world.

We hope that readers will enjoy trying out the activities in the book and find that their creative teaching inspires their young learners.

Part 1

Knowing and challenging your learners

1 Getting to know your learners

Every child is important and close observation of what children do in lessons helps teachers to make sure their learners are progressing in their language learning. Teachers need 'eagle eyes' to watch how each child is attending, understanding, and participating. But children are not just learners; they are daughters or sons, brothers or sisters, with their own personalities and interests. The teacher needs information about the whole child. All this information can then be used by the teacher to meet the learning needs of the child.

↓ OBSERVING YOUR LEARNERS

It is important to be aware of each child's participation and interest in learning activities. From time to time, sweep your eyes around the room during an activity, keeping a mental note of who is participating and who isn't. Don't worry if sometimes some children prefer to listen and watch (see chapter 3, page 19).

Try this ☞ **Focused observation of individuals**

Observe all the children in row one or group one in this lesson, and in row two or group two in the next lesson, and so on. Note the children who always lead an activity, and those who prefer to follow. Note the children who are quick to use new language, and those who prefer to listen. A checklist of skills and expected outcomes of the lesson is useful as it can be completed quickly.

'My room' pairwork	Finished the task	Used 'Have you got ...?' questions	Used four English colour words	Used furniture vocabulary from unit	Got English adjective order right
Harry	✓	✓	✓		
Hanna	✓		✓		
Ayesha	✓		✓	✓	✓
Ali			✓		
Ruby	✓	✓	✓	✓	✓

TABLE I.I   *Skills and outcomes checklist*

Try this ☞ Focused observation of groups

Set up group activities and walk around the room, stopping at each group. Encourage groups to continue with their activity even when you're watching and listening. Interact with the group and individual children, responding to children's interaction and participating without taking over. Support learning when help is needed and make a mental note of the help you gave.

Teacher: *Jon, what do you think?*

Teacher: *Have a guess.*

Teacher: *Tell me what you're trying to do.*

Teacher: *Carry on! I'll just watch for a while.*

Teacher: *When I come over, just keep working.*

Teacher: *Can I help you with that?*

Keeping a record of learners' participation and performance

While marks give some indication of how a child is progressing, other types of record of what has been done in an activity can give a deeper picture.

Whenever possible, write notes about children's participation and performance (in charts, in teacher notes, and on children's work). Table 1.2 shows an extract from a teacher's notes on five young learners.

Date	Activity	Anna	Freda	John	Philip	Teresa
5th Oct	Writing a zoo story	Short, but used a good range of vocabulary.	Needs work on past tense.	Has a good idea of narrative structure.	Poor – Missed the excursion, and preparation activities.	Needs more vocabulary work.
10th Oct	Vocabulary work (zoo)	9/10 words remembered	5/10	7/10	4/10	6/10

TABLE 1.2   *A teacher's notes on the progress of five children*

A little pad of pieces of paper with a sticky edge ('sticky notes') is useful. You can quickly write the child's initials and a comment on a sticky note and put it next to the child's name on a class list or in your record book. After class, you can write the comment more fully.

You can also give each child a portfolio in which to store their work and this can act as a record of their progress (see chapter 18, page 67).

↓ TALKING TO PARENTS TO UNDERSTAND THE CHILD

A good source of information about a child is their parents. You can ask parents about their child's interest in English and first language literacy at home. Here are some questions to consider:

- Does your child read books in her/his first language?
- Does he/she have a chance to talk to English-speaking people or watch English TV?
- browse existing tags
- Does he/she read books or other material in English at home?

Getting to know your learners

• Does he/she like learning English?

Use the child's portfolio of work as a reference for discussion with parents (see chapter 18, page 67).

Why this works

In the classroom, the teacher has the responsibility to make sure that each child is learning; it is not the responsibility of the child alone to keep up with what the teacher is teaching. Teachers therefore need to observe and note individual children's needs, and then work on meeting those needs through supporting their learning. Children bring different experiences and knowledge to their learning and it is likely children will each learn something different from the same activity.

Observation sheets for activities, prepared beforehand, help teachers to know what they are looking for. Record sheets help teachers to maintain an understanding of each child's progress, and to plan to meet children's needs in the future as well as to assess progress by looking back over a term or year.

Focused observations of the child's level of participation and emotional well-being help teachers to attend to the child's emotional and attitudinal needs, and parent interviews help teachers to understand each child's experiences, interests, and attitudes.

2

Expect a lot from your learners

Teachers know that children will do well if they expect lots from them – and they also know that children will do less well when teachers expect little from them. It is therefore important that teachers' expectations of children's learning are always high: realistic, but high. Keeping expectations high is not easy so we have to challenge ourselves as teachers to do this.

↓ HIGH EXPECTATIONS WITHOUT PRESSURE

There are various ways we can provide opportunities for our young learners to excel. It is not a question of putting too much pressure on young learners to achieve, but is a question of providing stimulating tasks for them to do, giving them lots of exposure to English, telling them what is expected of them, and praising their efforts.

Cognitively challenging tasks

Cognitively challenging tasks are problem-solving tasks and activities that involve knowledge about something other than language. Give lots of preparation and scaffolding (structured support) along the way.

Child: *We put the daddies together and the children together.*
Child: *We put all the squares together.*
Child: *We put the red ones here and the blue ones here.*

Try this ☞ Classifying pictures and shapes
Give children pictures from magazines, or shapes of different colours (and thicknesses if possible). Ask pairs or groups to classify them and say why they have classified them in this way.

Try this ☞ Maths problems
Set maths problems at children's level in their regular maths classes. Ask them to give their answer in English and talk about what they did to solve the problem.

Try this ☞ Mind maps
Make a mind map of everything children know about a new topic, for example, zoo animals, the weather, or ways to travel.

Providing lots of spoken English

A good way of challenging your learners is to speak lots of English (tuned to your young learners' level of proficiency) and expect them to understand.

- Use gestures and pictures to help them understand.
- In action games like 'Simon Says' (see chapter 3, page 19) make some of the actions and language more advanced than children's current language.
- Use translation into children's first language only as a last resort – it's best to use translation only for some new, difficult words.

Setting criteria for activities

By making a list of your expectations in the child's performance in an activity, you can be sure you are challenging each child. You can also use this to inform your observations (see chapter 1, page 12).

For example, you might be giving your young learners a barrier activity to do, where two children sit opposite each other with a barrier such as an open book between them. They are asked to find out information from each other, for example, they have slightly different pictures – each with some information missing – and have to find out what is different and fill in the gaps. By the end of the activity they should both have the same picture.

If you are going to give your learners a barrier activity to do, you might set the following criteria.

In the barrier activity, each child will:

- speak clearly
- remember not to speak too fast
- listen carefully
- ask their partner about something they don't understand
- not look at their partner's picture
- after 20 minutes, have found all the differences between the two pictures

Expect a lot from your learners

Try this ☞ **Let your learners set the assessment criteria**

If you are setting criteria for older learners, it can be helpful to involve the learners in developing the criteria which are going to be used to assess an activity. You can prepare criteria for discussion with your learners before the activity and agree a set of criteria with them which you write on the board. This involvement in how the task is assessed will boost your learners' involvement in the task.

Even with younger learners doing more simple activities, letting the learners know or choose one or two of the criteria can help make clear what you expect from them.

Teacher: *Remember not to talk too fast!*

Teacher: *Listen carefully to your partner.*

Teacher: *Speak loudly and clearly to your partner.*

Using praise

In order to encourage your learners, find something to praise in their work and show them models of work that meet your criteria. This could be the presentation of their work or the effort they have made if the English itself is not very good.

Teacher: *Is this the monster you've written about? Isn't he scary! What a good picture you've drawn!*

Teacher: *Your writing is very neat, Javier, well done. Now let's look at the spelling here: how do you spell 'face'?*

Teacher: *Thank you for showing us the photos of your cat and telling us about him. You spoke very clearly, Fatima, well done.*

Using extra language

Have you ever wondered if your learners could understand more than you offer them? Sometimes learners have experienced English outside the classroom and could benefit from extra teacher talk inside the classroom to stretch them. Sometimes their comprehension skills are more advanced than their speaking skills so that they could be hearing and understanding extra teacher talk.

Try this ☞ **Using extra language**

Extra language like *When you're ready* or *After you've finished* is valuable and it probably won't distract the children – they will be trying to work out what you want them to do.

Expect a lot from your learners

Choose some phrases to keep using over a period of two or three weeks, and see if any young learners start to use them themselves. Don't explain and don't test these phrases – they are just extra opportunities.

Teacher: *If you don't mind, …*
Teacher: *When you've finished, …*
Teacher: *As quietly as you can, …*
Teacher: *I want you to smile and …*
Teacher: *Please be very helpful and …*

You can also use extra language in instructions:

Teacher: *When you're ready, stand up and go to the board.*
Teacher: *When you've finished, put the pen down and go back to your seat.*
Teacher: *Use a pen to draw a smiley face.*

 ✓ *Getting it right*

Using extra language

What you are trying to do with extra language is work at the edge of your learners' capabilities, not swamp them with completely incomprehensible talk. They should be able to understand most of what you say, and be able to work out or guess the meaning of the 'extra language'.

Why this works

Research has shown that without doubt children (and adults too) will do better when teachers' and parents' expectations are high. If they are told they can do it, and if the teacher cheerfully encourages them to try, most children will do better than we think. But there is a careful balance for the teacher to achieve – the task must not be too difficult, and the expectations must not be too high. Teachers need to know children's abilities and in order to be able to select the best tasks (see chapter 17, page 64). It is important that we never punish children when they don't succeed. All children benefit most from praise, and especially from seeing models of what teachers expect from them.

Remember too that children can benefit from being exposed to the language 'around' the language they understand: if sometimes your classroom language contains full and natural-sounding sentences, your learners will be getting more exposure to spoken language. Hearing and understanding English is good preparation for speaking it. Some children, especially those who have extra lessons outside school, are ready for more English than other. By adding extra words and phrases, you give these children something new and more challenging to learn, which will help them stay motivated.

3 Giving your learners access to new language

Teachers rejoice when children begin actively to try to understand what is being said or what they are reading. Teachers need to make this happen by choosing activities that engage learners. These activities need to encourage your learners to guess or predict the meaning of language they hear, using contextual clues like gestures, facial expressions, movement, and the visuals and objects you show them. Children need to be allowed to take risks in their response to language.

↓ LET LEARNERS FOLLOW WITHOUT SPEAKING

It is important that children can listen and watch without fear of having to speak until they feel ready. Make sure that other children don't laugh when a mistake is made, and encourage a child when they have a try.

Try this ☞ 'Simon Says' with counters

Play Simon Says, the game in which children respond to commands which begin with the phrase 'Simon says' but not to those without the phrase. If children do the wrong thing, don't make them sit out but give them a counter or piece of paper. The winner is the person with the fewest counters at the end.

Teacher: *Simon says – turn around three times then touch your shoes.*
Teacher: *Simon says – don't sit down if you are wearing a hat.*
Teacher: *Sit down!*

Try this ☞ Use Total Physical Response

You can let your young learners respond to language without having to produce it by using some Total Physical Response (TPR) in your lessons. TPR involves you giving instructions for an action such as, *Stand up and close the door*, for your learners to do. You can use progressively more difficult actions to make it more challenging. Below are some examples of the language a teacher would use in a TPR activity.

Teacher: *Sarah, sit down.*
Teacher: *James, touch your head.*
Teacher: *Everyone, sit down then touch your head.*
Teacher: *Michael, stand up and go over to the door and touch it, then come back and sit down.*
Teacher: *Michele, find all the people in the class who are wearing something red.*
Teacher: *John, if you are sitting down, please stand up and touch your toes.*

Children can build up understanding and always know what they have to do. That way they have no excuse not to have a go. For example, if you are doing an activity that requires watching or listening to a recording, you could follow these stages:

- Get the children interested in watching or listening to the recording
- Read the title together
- Ask children what they already know about the topic and make predictions about what the text will be about
- Brainstorm the vocabulary children know on the topic and write the words on the board (perhaps in a mind map)
- Watch or listen to the recording
- Ask questions and write notes about what you heard
- Set the children an individual task related to what they saw or heard – draw a picture and write about it; write some questions for their friend to answer.

For older/younger children

The method of Total Physical Response is useful for all ages to check understanding of language.

Older children still need lots of gestures, accompanying pictures and objects and other supporting material to help them to understand new language.

Why this works

Even when children progress in their language learning beyond the beginning stages they will always encounter new language that they need to understand and learn. We always want them to try to make sense of language.

Research has shown us that at the very early stages of language learning some children go through a silent period. Although they are not speaking, they are learning through watching and listening. It is important not to force them to speak. Indeed, teachers need to engage all children in what is going on in the classroom, especially through activities that involve watching, listening, and physical response because all learners learn language this way to some extent. When we encourage children to guess or predict what is being said, and to participate, then we are engaging them in learning. We can see in their eyes if they are engaged. Children who sit back and look out of the window or away from the action are not actively engaged. Also, when we allow children to say nothing, or to take risks with their responses, they have a chance to try out their guesses or predictions and to learn some more. It is a teacher's responsibility to engage their learners and to give them a chance to take risks, because this is what language learning is all about.

4 Celebrate achievement

It can be really motivating for your young learners to realize that they are making progress in learning English. Knowing that their English is growing will make them proud of their achievements and ready to learn more.

↓ SHOW THE CHILDREN HOW MUCH THEY HAVE LEARNED

One way of tracking learning progress is to show the language learned on the wall. Another is to provide opportunities for children to see or hear themselves speaking. They may be surprised at how much they can do!

Try this ☞ Words on the wall

Cover the wall with all the words and phrases the children have learned since they started in their first year of English – you can enlarge and photocopy the vocabulary lists in the coursebook, teacher's book or syllabus. It will be fun, and will be revision, for the children to try to pick out words they remember and read them from the wall. You can add new words at the end of a unit.

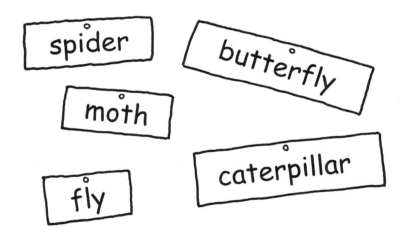

Try this ☞ New words list

Make a list at the start of the week of all the new words the children will meet. Tick off words on the list as they are understood and learned.

Teacher: *Look at all these English words that you know!*

Teacher: *This week we have learned ten words. Let's put them on the wall.*

Teacher: *Jasmine is speaking so clearly there.*

Celebrate achievement

Teacher: *Fred is really trying to find the words he needs. That's so good!*

Teacher: *Wow! See how much you've learned!*

Teacher: *Your English is getting so good!*

Try this ☞ **Videoing the children speaking**

Make a video of the children speaking English with confidence. Let the children practise and re-record if they want to. You can watch it together, giving huge amounts of praise for what has been achieved. If video equipment is not available, audio recording is a good alternative.

Confidence-building

You can boost your young learners' confidence in their English by preparing them for situations where they can use English, or where they have to provide help for someone who speaks less English than they do.

Try this ☞ **Preparation for an English-speaking event**

It's good for your young learners' confidence if you can prepare them for an English-speaking event, such as meeting another child on the beach on holiday; asking a question to a school visitor; or visiting another class. You can build up a sense of achievement by reminding the children afterwards of what they have learned and how they used the language.

Try this ☞ **Children as English experts**

Have the children help someone else to learn some English – it could be a puppet owned by the teacher, or a child from a lower class. Being the teacher or expert will make them feel motivated.

For older/younger children

Younger children are more centred in the here and now, and so less likely to be worried about the size of the task of learning English that lies ahead of them.

Older children have an advantage in that they can reflect on the process and on their achievements. Any visual way of recording the scale of their learning will help motivate. They also are able to conceptualize the years and months ahead of them and that they have spent learning, so that a sense of building up knowledge and skills should be more possible.

Why this works

Learning a language takes a lifetime; it is never finished with. This can be demotivating, especially for children who may think that learning English is like learning to ride a bike, learning to swim, or learning any of the other skills that are part of growing up. Discovering that there are always more words to learn, that they still can't say what they want to, and struggling to capture a foreign accent can decrease children's motivation but you can help by being as positive as possible about their efforts.

5 Let your learners experiment

Children who are given a chance to try out some new language may surprise their teacher with what they can do. It doesn't matter if children make errors when they try something new, because errors often indicate children are stretching their language knowledge. You can encourage your young learners to experiment and stretch their English through the way they ask and follow up questions.

↓ GIVING CHILDREN TIME TO THINK

Some ways of giving your learners space are as simple as giving them longer to answer after asking a question. If you give extra 'wait-time' after asking a question, they may try harder to answer.

Try this ☞ **Asking open-ended questions**
Open-ended questions often begin with question words such as *Why...?* or *How...?* They expect more than a yes/no or single word answer. If you use open-ended questions, your young learners will have to use more language.

Try this ☞ **Let children initiate a point in a discussion**
Listen to the children's ideas and respond to them, instead of always using the 'teacher's question and learner's answer' interaction pattern.

Teacher: *Look at this picture of a ....what is it? ... yes, a chimpanzee. Look at its long arms and hairy body. It's a mother chimpanzee.*
Anna: *Miss, baby, baby. On back.*
Teacher: *Yes, Anna, I think you're right. The baby is on its mother's back.*

Changing pace

Create opportunities for children to convey their own meaning in fast-paced activities, where you avoid correcting errors.

Try this ☞ **Catch**
Children stand in a circle and you throw a ball to one of them while at the same time giving them a word or topic, for example, *sports, Spain,* or *your house*. They have to say something about the topic when they catch the ball.

Let your learners experiment

Try this ☞ **Team games**

Play a team game: for example, each group has to answer a quiz about the animals (or another topic) that they have studied. Listen for factually correct answers rather than the accuracy of the language. The winning team has the most correct answers.

Stimulating children's imagination

Children have very active imaginations and will seize an opportunity to be creative in their English lessons.

Try this ☞ **Funny animals**

With your learners, describe 'the funniest animal in the world', drawing it on the board as you go through the description, or read a funny animal story or poem and ask the children to draw a picture about it. Your learners will enjoy being creative and surprising you.

For older children

Older children are likely to have more English that they have 'picked up' outside the classroom, for example, from using their computer, from TV, or from their holidays. This language may not appear in the coursebook and so it is good to give extra opportunities for the children to use it in class.

Why this works

When children have a chance to initiate what they want to say they have more opportunity to talk about what interests them, and to convey their own meaning. This helps their language to develop.

In first language learning, research has shown that parents ignore language errors in their young children's speech and are much more likely to respond to the accuracy of the meaning.

Child: *Daddy, I seed a pink elephant at the zoo today.*
Father: *How exciting! But did you really see a pink elephant?*

When they do respond to language errors, it is often through their response

Child: *We saw a dronkey too, didn't we Mummy?*
Mother: *Yes, we did, we saw five donkeys.*

Giving children the chance to say what they want to say (often with errors), and letting them try out language to convey what they want to say gives them confidence and develops their English.

Experiments on wait-time have shown that more extended and comprehensive answers are given by learners when teachers wait a little longer for answers.

Let your learners experiment

Part 2   Encouraging your students to learn

6   Recycling language

Don't just teach something once and then move on to the next thing. Recycling language means using the same words or phrases in new situations, and is not just helpful but also necessary for language learning.

↓ RECYCLING WORDS AND PHRASES IN DIFFERENT CONTEXTS

One way of recycling is to use words and phrases from the coursebook unit in different contexts. For example, in the classroom language below, you will see that the teacher is recycling vocabulary (*red coat, buttons, picture*), and grammar (*is wearing; let's;*) from many different past activities. The same words are spoken in different contexts: looking at pictures, playing with puppets, dressing up, drawing, and reading a story. In the last sentence, the phrase *who is wearing* is added as extra English to expose the children to more complex language (see chapter 13, page 52).

Teacher: *The boy in the picture is wearing a red coat with white buttons.*

Teacher: *Look! The puppet is wearing a red coat with white buttons!*

Teacher: *John, put this red coat on.* (John puts on a red coat in the classroom.)

Teacher: *Let's draw a picture of a boy in a red coat. Let's put some white buttons on the coat.*

Teacher (doing a story with pictures): *The boy who is wearing the red coat looks happy.*

Try this ☞   **Play 'spot the recycled word'**

Tell the children that you are going to use a word more than ten times in the lesson and they have to tell you what the word is by listening for it. For example, if you choose the word *banana*, you can use it in talk with the class, in a story or song, in commands that you give the children in games, and in counting activities. Children may notice other words that are recycled but not deliberately.

Teacher: *One, two, three, bananas.*

Teacher: *Children, please stand up. Now sit banana.*

Teacher: *Once upon a time there was a little banana who lived . . .*

Children like the familiarity of activities and materials that they know, and can benefit from repeating activities and from using familiar materials in different ways.

Try this ☞ **Recycling an activity or unit from the coursebook**

If you take an activity or unit from the coursebook that your learners did last term or last year and do it again with them, you might be surprised at what they do or don't remember. You may find that they remember it well and so have a chance to be fluent and expert, or you may find that they still have some things to learn from it.

Try this ☞ **Recycle favourite songs and games**

You probably already recycle your young learners' favourite songs and games but you can make recycling more helpful to learning by making small changes:

- Sing the verses of a song in reverse order, starting with the last.
- Sing a song silently, miming the words.
- Have a child be 'teacher' and give the commands of a game.
- Change a key word in a song. For example, replace 'bus' with 'lorry' in the song *The wheels on the bus*. Trying to remember the changed word each time will make the children concentrate, and make them laugh.

Try this ☞ **Recycle pictures and other visual aids**

Pictures and visual aids can be re-used in different ways to recycle the same language with a different activity:

- A video that the children know can be used for a game of 'What happens next?'. Stop the recording in the middle and ask the children *What happens next?*, collect some of their ideas, then watch and see if they were right.
- A comic strip that children have read can be cut up for children to put in order.

You can also re-use your materials to work on different language points:

- A picture that you used for action words can also be used for practising colours or shapes.
- A set of pictures of, for example, 'People who help us' can be used for comparisons (*The policeman is taller than the teacher*) and also for categorizing (*I have put the shopkeeper with the bus driver because they both work in town*).

Why this works

Young learners need to encounter words and phrases many times for them to become part of their vocabulary. Not only that, but children learn best by meeting language (and ideas) in different settings. Each time the language is used, children can learn something more about it.

Some children need more time and exposure than others to learn words and phrases, and recycling gives them sufficient exposure to the language, while the new contexts help maintain the interest of the other children.

Language and visual aids can be recycled from all kinds of past teaching activities and materials. This makes efficient use of the work that you put in to preparing lessons and materials.

7 Healthy competition

Friendly competition can motivate children to learn and use English. If activities are chosen well, children can be motivated to try a little harder, and will enjoy the activity more and learn something new. Children love to play games, but they hate to lose. Teachers of young learners therefore know that they need to take great care in the selection of games to avoid disappointment, while also teaching children how to win and lose graciously.

↓ GROUP ACTIVITIES

Putting young learners into teams for competition in the classroom can help them learn to work together, and belonging to a team can expose each child to less stress in the competitive situation.

You can consider giving each team a name, or let the teams choose their own name, such as Lions/Tigers/Leopards; or Stars/Planets/Moons.

For all competitive activities, it is important to explain at the beginning how many points you will give to the team that does best each time (and how many points to the other teams), and what the children need to do to be 'best' – it might be the fastest team to finish a task, the team to get the most answers right, the funniest role-play, or the clearest singing of a new song – the learners need to know what they're aiming for.

Teacher: *The winners are the team which finishes first – they will get three points. The second team will get two points, and the third team will get one. Are you ready?*

Teacher: *Well done everyone! So, the Tigers finished first. Three points to the Tigers . . .*

Teacher: *Let's see who can get the most right answers. They will get a point.*

Teacher: *Ok, everyone, time's up. Put your pencils down. Let's see who has got the most right answers . . .*

Teacher: *Let's sing the song again and this time I'll give one point to the team who sings most clearly. I want to hear all the words.*

Teacher: *I think that the Lions get a point for that. Well done, Lions!*

Try this ☞ **Board run**

Divide the class into two teams. Ask questions that help children to revise grammar such as plurals, irregular past tense, etc.
- *One sheep, two . . . ?*
- *Today we are running; <u>yesterday</u> we . . . ?*

The person at the front of each team runs to write the answer on the board. Other team members can whisper the answer to help the runner. The first correct answer wins a point for the team.

This game can also be done to revise vocabulary or content knowledge:

* *What is the name of a baby sheep?*
* *How many legs has a spider got?*

Teacher: *Joanne, you go into the Moons team. Lee, you go into the Stars.*

Teacher: *Moons, you go first.*

Teacher: *Ready, steady, go!*

Teacher: *The Stars won. Never mind, Moons.*

Teacher: *You tried very hard. Perhaps you'll win next time.*

Teacher: *Everyone tried very hard. Well done, everyone.*

Encouraging good behaviour through teamwork

You can use the same teams to encourage good behaviour in the classroom by rewarding good behaviour with a point. You can keep a large score sheet on the classroom wall where you mark the points for each team. At the end of the week or month, you can have a mini prize ceremony where you count all the points and find the winning team.

✔ *Getting it right*

Let all the learners belong to a winning team

When you organize teams in a class of young learners, it is important to monitor the teams' progress so that you can make sure that each child belongs to a winning team at some time in the term. As the term progresses, you can choose how you award marks to make sure that all teams have a chance to win. Good behaviour is as valid as good marks in English!

Teacher: *Which team can put their books away and sit down first?*

Teacher: *Who is going to be the best-behaved team today?*

Teacher: *Which team are going to be the best listeners today?*

Another way of using competition to help children to progress is to give a child a personal target to beat. Praise the child and encourage them, without pressure, to try to do even better next time.

Teacher: *See if you can get one more point in the test than last time.*

Teacher: *Ross, last time you scored 7. Let's see if you can get 8 this time.*

Teacher: *You did so much better this time! Next time, we'll try for 9!*

For older/younger children

Younger children are better at working alone or in pairs than as a larger team. By the age of six or seven, they can begin to work as teams.

Why this works

Playing games in the language classroom helps children to become motivated and to enjoy learning English. Competitive games also help children to develop skills in cooperating with each other and to be 'good losers'. Team games help to avoid children feeling bad if they do not win since in team games, the focus is taken away from the individual, and winning and losing is a more gentle and manageable experience for the young player. It is important that children's experience of learning English is as positive as possible, as they have many years of learning English ahead of them and we want them to stay motivated, not to give up early.

When 'competition' means striving for a personal best, a teacher's records and young learners' portfolios can help your learners to see how they have improved (see chapter 18, page 67).

8 Motivating young learners to speak English

We can help children to want to use English in the classroom. Children will automatically use their first language because it is easier for them, and because it feels natural. Using English will not feel natural but we can encourage use of English by providing both the language and the need to use it. Teachers also need to remind children about speaking English because they may forget in the excitement of doing activities and switch back into first language.

↓ EQUIPPING YOUR LEARNERS TO USE ENGLISH

In order for your learners to use English in the classroom in the way you want them to, they need to be able to produce useful phrases, and they need to be as comfortable as possible with listening to English. Below are some ways in which you can help them with this.

Try this ☞ **Using 'social English'**

You probably have taught your learners classroom English to use when talking to you (such as *How do you say . . . in English?* or *Can I have a (red pencil) please?*), but they can also benefit from knowing short phrases in English which they can use to talk to each other. This can motivate them to speak in English more. See Table 8.1 for some examples.

Function	Language
Asking for an opinion	*What do you think?*
Giving an opinion	*That's good.* *That's not right!*
Saying you have not heard or understood	*Pardon?* *What did you say?* *Can you say that again, please?* *Sorry, I don't understand. Tell me again.*
Taking turns	*Can I have a go?* *Do you want to have a go?* *Your turn!*
Setting boundaries	*Stop it!* *Wait a minute!* *Hurry up!*
Being polite	*Excuse me.* *Thank you.*

TABLE 8.1 *Social English for young learners in the classroom*

Motivating young learners to speak English

Try this ☞ **English-speaking teacher**

Try continuing to speak in English even when children don't fully understand the language. Use gestures, objects, or pictures to help them understand what you mean. Try talking in ideas, not just in single words.

Look at the man driving the train! He looks happy, doesn't he!

Children need to have both a focus on words (*man, train*), and phrases (*driving the train*), and to hear words in longer sentences. When they hear words in phrases and/or sentences, they are hearing and learning the important 'little' words that go with the nouns or verbs, like *the* or *at*. Keep increasing what you expect children to understand (see chapter 2, page 15).

Try this ☞ **Playing parrots**

For this activity you can either use your own voice or a recording, but choose a situation where there is expression in the speaker's voice, such as surprise or happiness. The idea is that the children repeat the sentences they hear, matching the natural speed and intonation. You can tell the children that for two minutes they are going to be like parrots, copying everything you say and the way that you say it. Let the children imitate you phrase by phrase, following your voice very closely. Try to make this as fast as natural speech and use natural intonation, so that it is more like 'shadowing' than like choral repetition. The children will probably exaggerate but that is fine; it is about them becoming aware of the rhythms and intonations of English.

Time for first language and time for English

Try this ☞ **Language robots**

Tell the children to pretend they have a switch on their shoulders, like a robot, which can be switched to English or to their first language. At the beginning of a lesson, or at points during a lesson when you hear lots of first language being used, remind them to *Switch to English!*

Try this ☞ **Mark the time for English**

Make a large poster with a moveable arrow to put at the front of the class. Turn the arrow to 'Only English!' when you want children to speak English only. Start with very short periods of 'Only English', and gradually extend the time as you observe children managing longer periods. Make it fun!

Try this ☞ **Two minutes of first language**

The idea here is to help children be more aware of which language they are using. A chance to use first language may also relax and revitalize the class. When you hear the children using mostly first language, stop the activity and give the children two minutes to speak only first language (and they must keep speaking to each other for the whole time). Time them with the clock or your watch, and announce loudly at the end of two minutes, *Now it's time to speak English again!* You can do this several times during a lesson.

Teacher: *Right! I want to hear only Cantonese for two minutes. Go!*
Teacher: *Stop! Now switch to only English. Go!*

Creating a need to communicate

Another way of encouraging children to speak English is to create a situation in which they want to tell you something. An example of this is 'Find the butterfly':

Try this ☞ **'Find the butterfly'**

Cut out a butterfly from coloured paper. Each day, before the children come into the room, stick the butterfly in a different place. The children have to find where the butterfly has landed. You will need to ask some prompt questions:

- *Where's the butterfly?*
- *Is it under the cupboard?*
- *Is it on the table?*
- *Is it on the ceiling?*

The children will enjoy the challenge of looking for the butterfly, and the activity will give them reason to practise prepositions and classroom furniture vocabulary in English. If you want to help your learners with vocabulary, you could stick labels on parts of the room and on classroom furniture for them to see.

To make this a vocabulary learning activity, write two or three words on the butterfly's wings all connected with flying, which the children can use.

- wings
- take off
- land
- crash
- high in the sky

If you make lots of butterflies, a new one can arrive each day. A little flock of butterflies will soon build up a useful list of words!

You could use a cloud instead of a butterfly if you think this would have greater appeal to your learners.

Why this works

Getting children to want to speak English in the classroom involves a lot of skilled planning on the part of the teacher. Sometimes teachers invent such interesting tasks that their learners use their first language because they want to get the task done. It's important to achieve a balance between the interest of the task and the language demands. If speaking English makes children feel insecure or embarrassed, then they won't want to try. Tasks and activities should give children a real reason to use English that they already know well enough to use, even if it isn't easy. They then need plenty of encouragement and praise. You can help children to listen and then to speak, at first though action responses (see chapter 3, page 19) and then through short answers. Gradually, your young learners can be encouraged to say (and listen to) more and more English.

9

Listening activities: something different

Learning a new language makes exceptional demands on listening skills, to hear new sounds and rhythms, and to catch meanings as they flow past in speech. Variety in types of listening activity will help children focus and stay motivated.

↓ ADDING SOMETHING EXTRA TO LISTENING ACTIVITIES

Just as with other activities, some variety from the normal routine will help your learners pay more attention. There are small but significant ways you can add something extra to the listening activities you do in class.

Try this ☞ **Changing the demands of listening tasks**

The teacher changes how s/he talks for part of an activity:
- Talk faster or more slowly
- Talk in a higher or lower pitch
- Change the speaker: use men's voices; women's voices; children's voices
- Change the accent: use native speakers from UK, Australasia, or North America; and use non-native speaker accents from different regions.

Try this ☞ **Record sounds for the topic or unit of your course**

If you can record sounds from the real world, using these sounds in the classroom can really appeal to your young learners' imagination. For example, if the topic is 'Transport', record the sounds of cars, buses, or trains. For 'Animals', go to the zoo or make animal noises yourself. For 'Family', record the sounds of the kitchen or typical family activities. The learners have to match sounds to pictures or words, or they have to tell you what is happening.

Try this ☞ **Secret instructions**

This activity will encourage careful listening in a fun way. Think of a simple instruction for the children to follow, such as *Smile and look happy*, or *Draw a big elephant next to a small tree*. The first time you say the instruction very quietly, and the children have to try to hear what is said and do what the message tells them – but they should not tell anyone. Repeat the message slightly louder, and then again several times, until all children have heard the message and have done what it says.

37

Listening activities are demanding for any learner of a second language, since once the language has been heard, it is gone. To boost your learners' confidence in their listening skills, you can do activities which teach them how to listen attentively. Before you do these, try sitting in various places around your usual classroom to see if you can hear the CD player and make out the words. If you can't, the children can't, and your listening activities will be wasted.

Try this ☞ **Comparing how to get silence in different languages**

When English-speaking teachers want a quiet classroom, they may tell the children 'shh!' What do you say in your first language? Share these different ways of 'shushing' with the children. Discuss what sounds they have in common and why this might be.

Try this ☞ **Listening for the pin**

There is an English idiom: 'It's so quiet you can hear a pin drop.' Have your children sit very still and quietly while you drop a pin behind your back – can anyone hear it? Teach the children to understand the phrase so you can use it (in a very quiet and calming voice) before starting listening activities.

> Teacher: *Listen to the pin drop.*
> Teacher: *Shhh!*
> Teacher: *I want you to be so quiet that we can hear a pin drop.*
> Teacher: *Shhhhh.*

For older/younger children

Older children can take on the teacher's role in some of the above activities, for example, saying messages for their peers in small groups.

Why this works

Being able to hear the sounds of the new language is really important and really demanding for learners.

Linguistically, children need to notice the sounds of English that are different from those in their first language(s). Very young children (under about four years) are particularly good at learning a new accent from listening and participating in talk because they are still 'flexible' phonologically. Children older than this can benefit from directed attention to sounds through game-like activities.

Many classrooms are noisy places and sometimes children are not able to hear recorded talk clearly enough to learn. Listening in a foreign language needs quiet and it needs hard work from the children. It will help learning if you calm the children down and make sure the room is as quiet as possible before you start an activity.

You should, always, expect children to listen to everything you say as the teacher – don't start talking until they are all looking at you and listening.

10 Meeting written English

For children who are learning to read and write in English, seeing written language around the room is a useful reminder of what they have learned or need to remember. This kind of 'environmental print' in the classroom helps children to gain more control over the language and more confidence to participate and learn.

Try this 👉 **Making posters**

You can make poster displays with your learners to focus them on specific letters and sounds. After showing children flashcards of words beginning with, for example, *cl*, list the words on a poster and add some short sentences and little pictures beside them.

Try this 👉 **Make a pronoun mobile**

Make a double-sided mobile to hang up in the classroom with all the personal pronouns hanging on it: *I / you / he / she / it / we / they*. Then, when you want to focus your learners' attention on the difference between *he* and *she*, you can show them how it is written by pointing to the word on the mobile.

Meeting written English

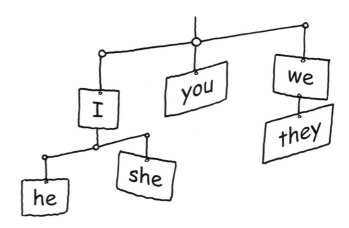

Teacher: *Remember we learned this word last week.*
Teacher: *Check the posters!*
Teacher: *Let's all look at the poster we did last week.*
Teacher: *Can you find 'she' on the mobile?*

✓ *Getting it right*

Making classroom displays

Make sure any text is large enough for children to read and not too high on the wall for small children. Keep the display fresh by taking the posters down when it is time for the children to remember the information without help. Keep renewing the posters, as children will stop noticing them after a while.

Try this  **Labelling parts of the room**

You don't have to stop at the putting writing up on walls: you can increase your young learners' exposure to written language by labelling the classroom furniture and parts of the room, such as *table, chair, door, whiteboard, floor*, etc. By seeing labels like *table* over and over again, with its meaning made absolutely clear, children will connect the word and the meaning, which will help them when they read and write.

Personalising classroom displays

Perhaps the best way of attracting children to the words and pictures you have on the classroom walls is to involve them in the making of the materials, so that the displays mean something to them. It could be something as simple as the children's artwork with their own English sentences written underneath (with help as necessary), or an interesting picture that you've found with sentences that your young learners have written in response to it.

Try this **Characters with speech bubbles**

If there is a storybook that is popular with your learners, you could photocopy and enlarge illustrations from it, and add speech bubbles so that the characters are saying phrases that the children have learned. It will increase children's interest if they help you decide what the characters are saying, so consider saving this part until the next class. The children will notice and read the writing on their walls.

Try this 👉 **Parts of the body posters**

If you have space, your young learners could make large posters of their own outline: working in small groups, one person lies down and the others trace carefully around them. Then the whole group can label the arms, legs, heads, etc., and the posters can go on the wall around the room.

Try this 👉 **Illustrating a short story**

You could try larger-scale projects once your learners know enough English, such as making up a short story together and writing it on a large poster, and sticking children's illustrations next to it on the wall.

↓ READ FOR MEANING

Reading takes many different forms in English language classrooms – reading aloud; reading all together in a chorus; reading individually and silently; reading and translating into first language. However, the central task of a skilled reader is to make English meaning from English written text, and children should experience this from the earliest stages of learning to read.

Try this 👉 **Put meaning at the heart of each child's reading**

This is known as the 'language experience' method or approach. Learners tell you what they want to read in English and you write it for them to read, for example, *I am going on holiday next week*. You can translate into English or help the child construct the sentence, but the meaning should be clear for the child because the idea came from them. The child reads the sentence, draws a picture about it, and could write the sentence as well. Over time, sentences and pictures can be put together to make a special book for the child.

Try this 👉 **Getting familiar with reading through storybooks**

Children love to hear their favourite stories again and again. When you use storybooks with your learners, the pictures should help the children to get the meaning of the story, but you can also help bring the story alive by making simple paper puppets of the characters in the story, such as Little Red Riding Hood, or the wicked stepmother in *Hansel and Gretel*. The children can make simple finger puppets from photocopies of the characters. As you read the story aloud, the story characters can move and speak. They can act out parts of the story – running away and hiding, asking questions, etc. Lesson by lesson, you can act out a small part of the story, first for the children and then with them, building up and consolidating the meaning of the whole story.

Let the children look at and play with the storybook and the characters. They may read (or pretend to read) the stories to each other. Even if they 'read' by re-telling the story from memory, they will still be learning the idea that the text tells a story.

Meeting written English

Try this ☞ **A reading corner**

If there is a corner space in the classroom that could be 'the reading corner', you can use this as an area where children can go and read when they have finished their work, or where they can choose something to take back to their desk. You can collect English books at the right level for your learners and place them on display in the reading corner. You could even make a class 'book' from a collection of children's illustrated writing on a common topic, such as, 'Things I like to eat'. Class books can be added to the reading corner.

Teacher: *Have you read each others' stories?*

Teacher: *Let's make a class book together to put in the English corner.*

Teacher: *If you've finished your work, you can go and find something in the English corner to read.*

For older/younger children

The same ideas will work for all ages. Older children who have learned to read and write in their first language before starting English will make faster progress, but still need the focus on meaning. Older children may prefer non-fiction to stories, such as books about dinosaurs, or transport, or history.

Very young children may have difficulty making the shapes of some English letters because their hand muscles are still developing. Using plastic letters to make words will be useful.

Why this works

Children do not instantly remember what teachers have taught them. Teachers know that learning takes place when children meet new ideas, words, and phrases several times and in different contexts. Putting language up around the classroom helps children to revisit what they have learned, either as the teacher points it out again or as they look at the language again in their own time. When written language is accompanied by pictures and objects, and when it is presented in a way that reminds children of something they did in relation to the language, this helps them to remember the meaning of the language.

To develop reading skills, children have to learn how to decode letters and words and turn them into sounds when they read aloud, but this is only one part of learning to read. The central act of reading is making meaning from written text. There is a danger that children learning to read in a foreign language may put all their effort into saying or pronouncing the words, at the expense of meaning. Children need teachers to show them how to work out meanings from English text and to show them that they think this is important.

11 Parental involvement

Parents play an important role in their children's learning of English. It is good if parents encourage meaningful and cheerful use of English rather than pushing English so much that children resist it. Parents can show children that English is a living and useful language, not just a subject to be studied at school. Even parents who speak very little English can do this by conveying a positive attitude and looking for opportunities for others to help.

↓ KEEPING PARENTS UP-TO-DATE

You can involve your learners' parents in their children's learning by inviting them in to the school, or sending home news about the activities their children have done with you in class.

Try this ☞ **Invite parents in to school**

There are plenty of opportunities for inviting parents to school. It could be to watch children's performances or see displays of their work, or to show the parents their child's portfolio and discuss their child's progress (see chapter 18, page 67). Parents can also be brought in to help with trips or activities.

Try this ☞ **Send home news about English**

Parents will appreciate communication from you about what their child is doing in their English class. You could write short notes (in the parents' language) on what the children have learned this week, perhaps including some suggestions on what parents can do to help their children's English: *This week we have learned about animals in Africa. If you see animals on TV, you could ask your child for the English word.*

Some schools have their own website or virtual learning environment (VLE) which parents, teachers, and learners can access using a password. If your school has one of these, you could organize for parents to subscribe to an email newsletter from school.

Try this ☞ **Send home materials in English**

There are various ways of sending home to parents materials that their children have used in class. For recordings of songs or stories used in class, you might be able to lend a CD, or send an MP3 file of it by email. If you are able to make recordings in class, you could use email or the school's VLE to send this to the parents.

Parental involvement

How parents can help

Parents can help their children to learn English in lots of ways. Having English books around at home, or taking their children to children's English internet websites will expose their children to more English in a fun and purposeful way.

Try this ☞ **Have an English book box**

Parents can be encouraged to have an English book box in the corner of one of the rooms at home. Books can be changed from time to time at the library, at school, or perhaps exchanged with other parents. Books should have lots of pictures and colour. A parent could ask an English-speaking friend to visit and read a book from the English box to your child, and they could read to their child from the English box from time to time, perhaps before the child goes to bed.

Parent: *Listen! They're speaking in English!*

Parent: *Look! This book is written in English!*

Parent: *Would you like to read an English book before you go to bed?*

Parent: *What does this mean?*

Try this ☞ **Support children learning English**

Just like the teacher, parents can praise and encourage their children when they speak, listen to, read, or write English. Outside school this is likely to be for a real purpose (not just for study), for example, pointing out English on the internet, on the TV, on posters and signs, and on labels in the supermarket

Try this ☞ **Let the child be the expert sometimes**

Parents can ask their child about English words or phrases that they don't understand, or ask them what they learned at school and then ask for some more explanation. Asking children to translate English for their parents is a positive way of reinforcing language learning.

Try this ☞ **Use English on long journeys**

As a way of entertaining their children on a long journey, a parent can play games with them in English. For example, the children recite the days of the week, numbers, months of the year, colours, etc. They could sing songs they know – teaching their parents! Parents and children can play 'I Spy' in English:

Child: *I spy, with my little eye, something beginning with B!*

Parent: *Bus?*

Child: *No.*

Parent: *Bicycle?*

Child: *No.*

Parent: *Boat?*

Child: *Yes!*

Why this works

It is very easy for children learning a foreign language at school to think that it is just another subject to be studied, and just more exams and tests that have to be passed. Hopefully, school makes language-learning interesting and does not have too many tests for young learners. The most helpful thing for children learning a language is to understand early that they can communicate and learn through the new language. At school they can learn this quickly if teachers use many of the strategies outlined in this book – for example, playing games in English, reading English books, doing drama and singing songs, and speaking English with English visitors (see chapter 22, page 81). Parents can also help their children to understand this by showing them how English can have meaning and be useful outside school.

However, parents also need to remember that children's language and literacy development in their home language provides a strong foundation for their English, and that English should never take a more important place in children's lives at home than their home language.

Part 3

Going beyond the coursebook

12 Making the most of the coursebook

A good coursebook can be a really good aid for teachers, helping to order teaching, providing ideas for activities, and being a source of helpful and stimulating illustrations. Teachers can also provide children with valuable extension activities to reinforce, recycle, and extend learning.

However good the coursebook is, it was probably not written especially for the children in front of you, who have their own unique interests and abilities. Some young learners can learn and understand more than is in the book; others will need extra help to learn what is in there. Some young learners will find the coursebook interesting; others will have different interests. By 'stretching' the book and adding extra activities, teachers can provide even better learning experiences for all the children. Remember that teachers know their young learners and their learners' interests better than the person who wrote the coursebook.

Try this ☞ **How much is different?**

Look at pictures of children in the book and discuss with your learners where the characters are different from them and where they are the same as them. For example, are the children in the book doing what your learners do or wearing the kind of clothes your learners wear?

Child: *There aren't any MP3 players in that shop.*

Child: *The woman needs a mobile phone.*

Child: *He's not wearing trainers like we do.*

Try this ☞ **Stop and question**

To keep your learners' attention when using the coursebook with them, try suddenly stopping: close the coursebook in the middle of reading a text or doing an activity. See what they can remember of what they were just doing.

Teacher: *So, Mary and Sam were in the shop.*

Teacher: *Who can remember what they bought?*

Teacher: *What were they carrying?*

Teacher: *Who did they talk to?*

Try this ☞ **Random recall**

Try opening the book at random at a previous lesson to see what the children can recall. Most learners will benefit from the reinforcement and will enjoy the familiar language and activities.

Try this ☞ **Repeat a lesson**

You could let the children choose a previous lesson to do again, rather than a new one. As with random recall, they will enjoy the familiar language and activities.

Try this ☞ **Change mode**

Surprise your young learners by changing mode: turn a text into a song or a chant; or change a dialogue into a story or a performance. You could make a list into a letter, or a letter into a story.

Try this ☞ **Go electronic**

Rather than letters, children today write emails to each other, or communicate by text message. You could appeal to your young learners' imagination by asking them to pretend to be one of the characters in their coursebook and writing emails to each other in character.

Try this ☞ **Swap activities**

If there is a game or exercise that the children really enjoyed in a previous unit, adapt it for language in a new unit to replace an activity that is not very suitable for your learners.

Getting the most from pictures in the coursebook

Your coursebook can be a good source of pictures. From cartoons to photo stories, there is a lot of visual material to exploit, and the advantage of visuals in coursebooks is that all the learners will have their own copy of the picture.

Try this ☞ **The story behind the picture**

Use the picture as a starting point to make up a story, for example:
- Give a name to the girl in the picture.
- Give her a family, a home, a school, hobbies.
- Explain why she is on her own.
- Tell me how she came here.
- Where is she going next?
- What is she going to take with her?
- What is that dog going to do?

Write the story together on the board, or write up key phrases that children use to write the story.

Try this ☞ **Acting out a picture**

Children take on the characters in the story, and use chairs and desks to construct the setting. First compose the picture as a still image. Then start it moving and act out the story.

Supplementing the coursebook

As the teacher, you probably already supplement the coursebook in the following ways:

- words and phrases – extra vocabulary for faster learners.
- content – more ideas for interest.
- pictures – for more support and more interest.
- activities – for extra reinforcement or more fun.

Here are some more ways to get the most out of your coursebook by supplementing the activities and materials.

Try this ☞ **Extra material created by your learners**

Your learners can also add material, and it will reinforce their language. For example, in a unit on animals, they can draw animals that are not in the coursebook and write about them in captions, or in longer reports if they are more advanced. There may be a model in the book they can follow. They can bring pictures from home and tell the class about them before adding them to a display.

Try this ☞ **Older learners as authors**

If you teach a range of ages, you could ask your older learners to write, edit, or supplement a coursebook unit for a younger class. They are likely to have some good ideas for interesting activities or for adding pictures to give extra support to new language. They are also likely to respond enthusiastically to being asked their opinions about coursebooks.

Why this works

The coursebook is intended as a resource for the teacher. In the early years of a teaching career, and beyond, coursebooks can give a framework and structure for teaching. A confident teacher will feel able to evaluate the coursebook and ask critical questions about how well it suits the children in terms of:

- the amount of language included in a unit
- the support for children to understand the meaning of language
- the usefulness of the activities
- the sequencing and building of language
- the recycling of language.

Over the years, you will come to see what works well and what works less well in the coursebooks you use. You will develop a range of your own activities and materials that can be added to the book or used to replace things that don't work so well.

13 Surprising your learners

Once you have established your relationship with a class and they know how they should participate in your lessons, some little changes can make all the difference. Making changes in how you organize and manage the classroom can help to keep children motivated and interested. There are all sorts of small changes you can make from time to time – in the classroom, in your talk with the children, in activities, and in the objects you use.

↓ VARYING THE ROUTINE

Here are some different ways for adding variations to different aspects of your lesson. Just one change at a time is all you will need to keep things interesting. Too many changes may make your young learners feel insecure.

Try this ☞ **Change the classroom layout**

You could change the seating for one lesson in a week – if the children usually sit in groups, why not put them in rows, or move the chairs away from the desks? Could you all sit on the floor instead of at tables?

You could position yourself in a new place – if you usually sit or stand at the front of the room, lead an activity from the back of the room instead. The children who sit there will pay extra attention!

Try this ☞ **Change how you look – and see if the children notice**

You could wear a hat to class, or put coloured laces in your shoes, or a flower in your buttonhole.
- You are not trying to look silly but to surprise the children into speaking, and speaking in English.
- Both younger and older children can enjoy playing 'spot the difference' with the teacher.

Try this ☞ **Sing what you usually say**

If you are comfortable with singing, you could sing the register or the alphabet. You could speak a song that you usually sing.

Try this ☞ **Change your voice**

You could change the way you talk to the children for part of a lesson. Try talking in a (loud) whisper or quiet voice, so that the children have to really concentrate to hear what you say.

Try this ☞ **Show pictures or flashcards upside down**

The children can try making sense of pictures or flashcards upside down before you turn them the right way up. Do this several times before going back to the usual positioning.

Try this ☞ **Change a familiar story**

You can miss out some words when telling a well known story or change the names of the characters: put Goldilocks into 'Little Red Riding Hood' or put the Gingerbread Man in Cinderella's kitchen. Act surprised when the children notice the 'mistake' and ask them to tell you if you do it again – which of course you will!

Child: *Miss, you said Goldilocks! It's not! It's Little Red Riding Hood!*

Teacher: *Oh, silly me! I mixed them up. Tell me if I do it again. 'One day, Goldilocks . . .'*

Child: *Miss, you did it again!*

↓ ADD A LITTLE EXTRA LANGUAGE TO CLASSROOM TALK

Children can listen and respond to more complex language than they can produce. You can offer them the opportunity to hear more English than they can use themselves.

Try this ☞ **Tell the children about a picture using extra rich language**

Bring in a picture or a photograph that has lots of detail and interest to show the children. Talk about the picture; begin with the key words and phrases as you would normally do, but then add more language (see the long sentences below). Talk about what can be seen, and what people are doing or wearing. Give lots of details but include some familiar words and phrases for the children to notice. Point to what you are talking about. Keep the overall talking time quite short.

Teacher: *Look – here's a picture of the seaside. There's a house and a shop. There are two men in a boat. The shop sells fishing nets that the fishermen take to sea to catch all kinds of fish for us to eat. The boat has a large engine at the back to make it go really fast in case a storm starts. It's been painted dark, yellow-ish green . . .*

For older/younger children

Children's capacity to be surprised changes with age. For very young children, much of what happens is new and surprising, so they usually prefer a more settled regime in the classroom. When you make changes in the routine of very young children, keep them small and infrequent.

Older children from seven years old upwards will enjoy little surprises much more than the younger ones. You can also involve older children in planning (nice) surprises for their fellow learners and let them suggest ideas too.

✓ *Getting it right*

Be consistent with young learners

While small changes to established classroom routines can be effective at keeping children's attention, it is important to remember that children benefit from predictable teacher behaviour. If you tell the class that you will do an activity, it is important that you do it. If you make promises, keep them. If you tell children what will happen if they break your classroom rules, then it is important that you carry this through. If you are not consistent, the children will feel insecure and this can lead to bad behaviour.

Why this works

We are not suggesting that the classroom becomes an unpredictable place but that surprises embedded in a secure and comfortable routine can liven up a predictable classroom climate. If every lesson is the same, with the same types of activities in the same order, the children will be bored and their attention may drop. We know that focus and attention is necessary for learning. So, making some small but surprising changes every so often will help keep the children 'on their toes' and ready to learn.

14   Using your hands

Teachers are often very good at helping children understand English, especially with their hands, making gestures with their hands to show the meaning of what they are saying, to encourage learners to speak, and to show who should speak. Gestures supplement the pictures you hold up on flashcards or draw on the board. While use of your hands is necessary, sometimes it can be helpful to consider how much English your learners actually need to understand you. Are your young learners learning your sign language instead of your spoken language?

Try recording and watching yourself on video to see what your hands do in English lessons. Set up a video recorder on a tripod at the back of the room, or ask a colleague to record you. Watch the video and see how often you use your hands, and what you do with your hands. How do your actions help the children to understand English and to know what they have to do? Could you do more? Could you do less?

Try this ☞ **Use your hands to remind children**

A familiar gesture can be a quick way to give children feedback or help:
- Pointing behind you and raising your eyebrows can remind a child to use the past tense rather than the present.
- A child who has forgotten a word may remember when you use the gesture that you used when you first taught it.

Try this ☞ **Use your hands more effectively**

Informed by watching yourself, try to make your gestures more precise.
- If you want to show something big, make it really big.
- If you want to show something round, make it clearly round.

Watch how actors or children's TV presenters use their hands; pick out a new technique to try in class.

When planning a lesson or some new language, think in advance about
- which particular language you will use gestures to illustrate
- what kind of gestures can help understanding of this language.

Consciously reduce use of your hands as children become familiar with words and phrases so that you do not support what does not need supporting.

'No hands' English

In some classrooms the teacher does so much work with their hands that the children can probably understand everything without using any English at all.

Try this ☞ **No hands**

For part of a lesson, put your hands behind your back and hold them there. Let the children listen to what you say, not watch what you do. This may be difficult for you and for the children. If it is very difficult, then you are probably using your hands too much.

Why this works

If children are to learn words and phrases in English, they need to hear what you say and work out the meaning of what you say. From their experience of learning to understand in their first language, they have some good strategies for predicting what adults mean: they look at gestures and at things in the environment and guess what is being said.

If the children have problems understanding your 'no hands' English, you may be using English that is too difficult for them, or they may have stopped listening to the English you use and be relying only on your hands to explain things and tell them what to do. If you're too good at gestures, you may be giving too much support. However, conscious and deliberate use of hand gestures can be very helpful to children in understanding new language or remembering what they learned earlier. Gestures that support meaning can be gradually reduced as children come to understand the words or phrases.

Part 4

Empowering your learners

15 Let the children choose

Teachers and parents know that when children make a choice they are more likely to engage with that choice. Having a choice helps children to be motivated and to take responsibility for what they do, and this leads to learning.

↓ BUILDING IN CHOICE

There are many ways that teachers can build in choice into everyday teaching and learning activities. Children can be given a choice of topics, activities, friends to work with, and order of activities. Even the smallest kind of choice can enliven lessons and motivate learners.

Try this 👉 **Give children a choice of who to work with on an activity**

Ask your learners to find three people to work with as a group; or let them choose between working alone or with a partner. If you have class groups, take one person out of each group and let them choose a new group to work with. This type of change will help keep groupings fresh and prevent the formation of cliques.

Try this 👉 **Ask the class to choose the order of activities**

Sometimes it will be appropriate to involve the class in making choices about what they do. They might choose which one of two activities in the coursebook they would like to do next, or which of several activities they would like to do today and which tomorrow. Or each learner might choose the order in which they write down a list of words to take home to learn.

Teacher: *Which activity shall we do next?*

Teacher: *Choose a partner to work with.*

Teacher: *You can work on your own if you like.*

Teacher: *Would you like this one or this one?*

Try this 👉 **Give children a choice of what to say**

Instead of giving children ready-made pictures for activities, give them a list of items to include in a picture, and tell them that their homework is to draw a picture including the items. Drawing the picture for homework saves valuable lesson time for speaking. In the next lesson, the children can then use their pictures in a barrier activity (see chapter 2, page 16), dictating their picture to a partner for them to replicate it, or finding differences between their pictures.

Learner 1: *Put the duck in the pond.*
Learner 2: *Yes, it's sitting in the pond.*
Learner 1: *The tree is next to the pond.*
Learner 2: *OK.*
Learner 1: *The baby is under the tree.*

Try this ☞ **Have an English activity corner**

It doesn't have to be a corner, but if you have an area of the room designated for English activities and games, children can go there to choose something to do after they have finished their set work. You can have games and activities like Bingo, card games, matching games, and reading activities.

Teacher: *Do you want to read the poetry book or the book about the car?*
Teacher: *When you have finished your work, you can write a message to your friend.*
Teacher: *Who would like to go next?*

Why this works

All parents and teachers know that most reluctant children can be persuaded to do something when they are given a choice. Being in school automatically limits the choices available to children – they have to study what is given. Even in a situation with a tight curriculum or assessment schedule, small choices can be given, and can be motivating for children as a change from being told exactly what to do.

Choice must not mean that children choose something too easy for them. With care, teachers can limit the choices so that all choices that children can make are possible and appropriate for their learning.

If you include challenging choices, you may find that children actually choose something difficult rather than something easy. You will find out more about individuals by seeing the kinds of choices that they make.

16 Young learners as language detectives

Children's natural curiosity can be used to help them discover patterns in the grammar and vocabulary of their new language.

We discover patterns from noticing what is repeated and what is different. It is the contrast between what is repeated and what is different that tells you what comes next in these sequences:

xx ooo xx ooo x …?

cat ➔ cats   book ➔ books   chip ➔ …?

Learning from patterns continues into adulthood and is a key ability that we can use in the classroom.

↓ LISTENING FOR PATTERNS

A lot of material used for teaching children contains lots of repetition, which is useful for learning, as it helps children learn things through playful activity. But repetition does not have to be subconscious – it can be useful and fun to do activities with the children that focus them on the patterns that are repeated in phrases and in songs. This can be before the learners can write, when they are using a lot of rhymes and songs. Once the children have started to write, they can do pattern-detecting activities to bring together the spoken and the written English they know.

Try this ☞ **Exploring the language of songs and poems through listening**

In a song or poem, some words and sounds are repeated, while others are changed. As the class sings, children put up their hands each time they hear a particular sound or word, for example, *round* in *The wheels on the bus*, or *monkey* in *Five little monkeys*. The need to listen and respond physically will reinforce the patterns of the repeated words. A more advanced task is to do the same for rhyming sounds at the ends of lines, for example, *said, head, bed* in 'Five little monkeys'.

Teacher: *When you hear the word 'round', put your hand up.*
(sings) *The wheels on the bus go round and round,*
Round and round, round and round.
The wheels on the bus go round and round
All day long.

Teacher: *Let's sing 'Five little monkeys'. Are you ready?*
(sings) *Five little monkeys jumping on the bed*
One fell off and bumped his head
So Momma called the doctor and the doctor said
No more monkeys jumping on the bed!

Four little monkeys . . .
Three little monkeys . . .
Two little monkeys . . .
One little monkey . . .

No little monkeys jumping on the bed
None fell off and bumped his head
So Momma called the doctor and the doctor said
Put those monkeys back in bed!

Try this ☞ **Same word**

Children enjoy playing with the words of phrases that they know by heart, for example, *Good morning; How are you?; My name is . . .* As in the other activities in this unit, the secret lies in helping children to notice the patterns of the English. You say the just first word of a phrase and let your young learners try to find or think of other phrases that begin with the same word:

- *Good morning; Good evening; Good bye; good work*
- *My name is . . .; My address is . . .; My dog's name is . . .*
- *How are you? How old are you? How tall are you? How many . . . ?*

↓ SHOWING PATTERNS IN WRITTEN ENGLISH

When children are learning to read, they can benefit from activities which make visible the connections between letters and sounds.

Try this ☞ **Showing rhymes in songs**

Write the words of familiar songs on large posters. Choose songs where the rhyming words are spelt in a similar way, e.g. *wall, fall* rather than *head, said*. Make sure the lines of the song fit the paper, so that rhyming words come underneath each other. Use colour to highlight the rhyming syllables, so that children can see the patterns of letters and sounds.

Try this ☞ **Word cards**

This is a written extension of 'Same word' above, where the children are producing more examples of phrases using a particular word. Once children are learning to read, each word can be written on cards for the children to use. With your guidance, your learners can place phrases containing the same words underneath each other to show the patterns:

- How / old / are / you ?
- How / tall / are / you ?

Young learners as language detectives

The word cards can be rearranged to show how questions connect to statements:

- How / old / is / she ?
- She / is / 10 years / old.

Try this ☞ **Collecting English translations**

There are many sources of texts that are in the first language and also translated into English:

- instructions for electronic gadgets, for example, CD players, cameras, computers
- labels on food packets or jars
- tourist information in leaflets or on the internet.

Children can compare the texts and their visuals in the two languages. Listen to what they find interesting. They may notice that the same word is used in both languages, or that very different words are used.

For older/younger children

Younger children will enjoy noticing sound patterns and rhymes, and it is important that we take advantage of young children's early abilities to hear different sounds. Older children need to learn how the sounds of English words rhyme for their reading skills but they can also learn from working with written English.

Why this works

Noticing and remembering patterns is a basic human ability that underlies much of our learning. Babies a few days old can learn the pattern of their mother's face and even before birth seem to recognize the pattern of their mother's voice or of music that is played to them regularly. Most five-year-olds can find patterns in numbers and colours. Most important for us, encouraging children to use their pattern-finding skills can help language learning through finding and using patterns of sounds and meanings.

Part 5

Assessment

17 Supportive assessment activities

Good classroom assessment activities enable children to show their teacher and their parents what they can really do. As well as finding out what young learners get right or wrong, we can assess children by finding out what kind of help they need and how much they can do for themselves. Good assessment activities make children feel good about what they can do, and encourage them to learn more. In order to set up a positive assessment activity, we need to consider how assessment activities can make the starting point the child, instead of the demands of testing and the curriculum.

Try this ☞ **Using support to assess what children can do**

In a classroom assessment activity, you can move around the class and help children who need help, and make a note of the support they were given. What children do with your support is a good indication of what they will soon be able to do alone. Here is an example:

- find a poem suitable for your learners' level of English, illustrated with a picture
- talk about the picture and read the poem to your learners for them to follow
- ask your learners to read the poem to themselves, saying the words in their head
- put your learners in pairs and ask them to read the poem to each other
- go around and watch and listen, and give help if they get completely stuck
- give the children a chance to help each other, and make a mental note of which children have helped and in what way.

Try this ☞ **Starting with easy assessment items that all children can do**

As a general rule when constructing tests such as grammar and vocabulary quizzes, reading tests, etc., put the easiest questions at the beginning of the test so that your learners can get warmed up to the difficult test. Gradually make the questions more difficult. Before the test, encourage your learners to try their best but help them to understand that some questions may be difficult and that this is alright.

The results of the test or quiz will show you what you still need to teach and to whom.

Try this ☞ **Use differentiated assessment activities**

Differentiated assessment activities give each child the chance to succeed at their own level of ability. An example for older or more advanced learners could be writing an account of an excursion that you have been on as a class:

- Talk to the children afterwards about what you did and what you saw.
- Write about the excursion together, composing an account of the excursion on the board. You can point out words and sentence structures for the children to use or copy that will help them to write their own accounts later.
- Then, rub off the shared account on the board, and ask the children to write about their excursion, reminding them of the features you hope to see.
- Assess each child's written account only after all this help has been given. (Take away your support at this point if you can, and make sure nobody copies.)

The structure that this activity has gives each child the chance to work at their own level of ability: it gives security and support while allowing freedom for each child to add their own language.

Teacher: *You can all do this activity!*

Teacher: *Now have a go yourself.*

Teacher: *Remember this is your story.*

Teacher: *Try your very best and show me what you really can do.*

Try this ☞ **Following up writing activities with help and support**

When you have collected in and marked a writing activity, pick some examples to show to the class as a model of good work. From marking the class's work, you will also be able to identify areas which were problematic for your learners: these are most likely to be difficulties with spelling or with sentence structure. You can go through examples of errors on the board with the class, asking the class if they can tell you the correct spelling or grammar, always being sure never to name who made the mistake.

If possible, talk to individual learners on a one-to-one basis about their work, pointing out where they have done well and what they need to work on. Keep it positive, and encourage them to keep trying by showing them where their previous efforts have paid off (see chapter 18, page 66).

Why this works

An assessment activity that engages all your learners and gives each a chance to succeed in some way is educationally sound and likely to result in more learning. When an assessment activity makes some children think 'I can't do it' and then stop trying, this is damaging to the learning process. Using assessment activities that are too difficult can cause children to lose confidence and motivation. On the other hand, if all parts of an assessment activity are too easy, we get a 'ceiling effect': some children can do far more and are not properly assessed. We don't want to trick children with difficult tasks so that we can sort them into weaker and stronger members of the class: we want to encourage learning, and to find out what each child's strengths and needs are. Assessment activities therefore need to include parts that everyone finds difficult, and teachers need to explain to children that it doesn't matter if there are parts they can't do in this activity. The impact can be reduced by having different activities at a range of levels and giving children the activity nearest to their capability.

18 Self-assessment works

It takes time and support to learn to assess your own work, but children can start young. When children participate in self-assessment, they begin to take some responsibility for their own learning and to develop a sense of autonomy or ownership of their work, which will motivate them to work hard. Self-assessment can help learners understand what makes a good performance or a good piece of work, which will in turn help them to achieve this.

↓ GETTING CHILDREN STARTED IN SELF-ASSESSMENT

Self assessment starts with small things, such as asking children to mark or grade themselves the end of a lesson or activity for participation and for work. This can be as a class or individually.

Teacher: *Did you work well today?*

Teacher: *What was good about how you worked today?*

Teacher: *What was not so good?*

Teacher: *What could you have done better?*

Teacher: *Should we get seven or eight out of ten for today's work?*

Try this ☞ **Using a checklist**

Try giving children a checklist of the characteristics of a good piece of work to start them thinking how they can assess their own work. See Table 18.1 for an example self-assessment checklist for the activity, 'Interview with a friend':

Task: An Interview with a Friend In this activity I will:	
● Write five questions to ask my friend. (Examples: How old are you? What food do you like?).	
● Ask my friend these questions and write down his/her answers.	
● Write a short description of my friend.	
● Include a photograph or a drawing of my friend.	
● Check that there are no grammar or spelling mistakes.	
● Ask a classmate to check my work.	

TABLE 18.1   *Young learner's self-assessment checklist*

Make sure the children understand the checklist. You will probably need to translate instruction words such as *check*, or *interview*. Explain the checklist and model how to use it, and then after they have finished, talk to individual learners about their experience of using the checklist.

Child: *I can't . . . but I can . . .*
Child: *I need to learn to do/say/spell . . .*
Teacher: *What makes a good piece of work?*
Teacher: *What language do you need for this task?*
Teacher: *Have you checked your work carefully?*

Try this ☞ **Prepare checklists together in class**

After some experience with checklists, teacher and children can prepare checklists together, so that the children share in setting criteria by which the work is assessed. This involvement will motivate them, as it increases their ownership of the assessment tool itself: it is not only the teacher who says what is good! After your learners have used their checklists, you can discuss how it was and together as a class change them so that they are better the next time they are used.

Try this ☞ **'Can-do' statements**

You can ask the children to evaluate what they can do in English at the end of term. See Table 18.2 for an example of 'Can-do' statements.

My name .... My class .... My teacher			
Things I can do in English			
	☺ **Yes**	☹ **No**	😐 **Mostly**
I can describe the objects in my classroom			
I can understand what my teacher asks me to do in class			
I can read and understand the stories chosen by my teacher			
I can ask my teacher for help			
I can …			

TABLE 18.2   *'Can-do' statements*

Using portfolios for assessment

A portfolio is a collection of a learner's work, held together in some kind of file or folder. The learner is responsible for filling their portfolio with their best work and, with their teacher, evaluating their progress at the end of the term or school year. Portfolios work very well with young learners since the process of selecting their best work to put into a portfolio encourages the children to take pride in their work. The teacher guides the learners' self-evaluation by encouraging them to use checklists and 'Can-do' statements to reflect on what they have learnt. The guidance can also be general questions which encourage children's opinions, such as *What is your favourite piece of work?* and *Why do you like it?*. The process of collecting work and reflective self-assessment helps learners see their own progress, while allowing the teacher to monitor the progress of individual learners.

Try this ☞   **Helping each child to collect their work into a portfolio**

It will help their motivation if your young learners have some choice about what goes into their portfolios. To facilitate this, give each child a checklist of the type of items that should be placed in the portfolio, and the order in which they should be there. If they need more guidance, give each learner several samples of their work to choose from. For example, you can give the children their writing from four lessons and ask them to decide which is best, or neatest, or most correct, or most interesting. In the list below, the children can choose their three favourite pieces of writing and their favourite recording of their voice:

Things in my portfolio
1   My name, my class, and my teacher
2   My project on animals
3   A recording of me speaking
4   Three pieces of writing from this term
5   A list of books from the reading corner that I read this term
6   My self-assessment.

Give children the responsibility to check themselves that all these items are included and are in the right order.

If your school has the equipment available, electronic portfolios can be made on the computer by scanning in written work and pictures, and recording spoken English. They can be made available to parents electronically too.

For older/younger children

Older children can deal with more detailed criteria for tasks. They can also talk about the kind of language that is needed.

Younger children can use simpler criteria such as smiley faces for activities they liked or did well.

Why this works

The purpose of self-assessment is not to replace the teacher's judgement of the child's performance, but primarily to build up skills of self-evaluation and to encourage responsibility for learning. Children need to be trained to do self-assessment. You can work out the assessment criteria with your learners to build up their awareness of what they need to do to complete a task well. Simple ways of talking about assessment can be developed, especially in older children, as they talk with the teacher about the language that is needed to complete the task.

Part 6   Playing with the sounds of English

19 Internal English and English for play

↓ ENGLISH IN YOUR HEAD

Encouraging children to echo the English words they know internally – 'talking in their heads' – will help them learn the language and give them a strategy they can use inside and outside the classroom.

Try this 👉 **Demonstrate what we mean by 'talking in your head'**

Show the children how they can 'talk inside their head' by first saying a sentence out loud and then using exaggerated gestures and expressions to look as if you are saying it in your head, silently.

If children are familiar with the convention of speech bubbles and thought bubbles as used in comics, these can be used too. Make a large version of a speech bubble and a thought bubble with the same sentence in each. Hold up the speech bubble and speak the sentence. Hold up the thought bubble and say nothing at all but mime being thoughtful.

Explain in the children's first language that 'talking in your head' can be really helpful because it helps them prepare what they are going to say before they start speaking, which will make them sound more confident.

Try this 👉 **Share English words and phrases your learners enjoy saying**

Share the words and phrases. Then say them all together as a class, louder and louder, then softer and softer, and finally with no sound at all 'in the head':

Teacher: *What do you like saying?*
Child: *I like saying 'abracadabra' because it rolls around my mouth.*
Child: *I like saying 'My name is Sharon' because I know it well.*
Child: *I like saying 'Five brown hens eating corn' because it makes a nice picture in my head.*

Try this ☞ **Use 'talking in your head' with different activities**

As a response to hearing the teacher or a recording, ask the children to repeat a sentence or phrase in their heads. Leave a pause while they do so, then have them say it aloud. Emphasize how much better it sounds after saying it in their heads first. As preparation for speaking, ask the children a question and tell them to say the answer in their heads several times, and then to tell the person sitting next to them. After the children have heard a text aloud, encourage them to read it 'in their heads' and then to read it aloud to their partner.

↓ ENGLISH FOR PLAY

The time that children spend in class with their English teacher is limited. If they learn things in class that they can use when they are at home and talking to themselves, the time that they spend with English will be increased.

We know that children spend a lot of time talking to themselves – when they play and create pretend worlds – as teacher, doctor, parents, etc., and when they lie in bed before going to sleep, or when they wake up and everyone else is still asleep. This talk is private, relaxed, and important for first language development. We don't know if children will use English in this way, but we can offer them the opportunity.

Try this ☞ **Counting backwards**

Show the children how to do this. Write the numbers on the board, going upwards from 1 to 10. Then start at 10 and move downwards, pointing to the numbers as you go. Challenge the children to do it. Then suggest that they try it at night in bed. And ask them to tell you what number they can start from tomorrow. If that's too easy, they can try these:

- say the alphabet backwards: z, y, x . . .
- count in twos: 2, 4, 6, 8 . . .
- count from 200: 201, 202 . . .

Teacher: *Who can count backwards from 10?*
Teacher: *Go on, Wendy. You try . . . Well done!*
Teacher: *Now who can count backwards from 15?*
Teacher: *You could count backwards when you are in your bed tonight.*
Teacher: *Tell me if you can count backwards from 20.*

Try this ☞ **Sing English songs at home**

Encourage the children to sing the English songs they know at home. Remind them of the songs they have learned with you and ask which their favourites

Internal English and English for play

are. They might want to do their favourites with you again in class. Once they know a song properly, they are more likely to sing it to themselves.

Try this ☞ **Telling a bedtime story**

When you have told or read the class a story, why not suggest that they can tell it to a little brother or sister, or to themselves, when they go home. They may well try to do this in English.

Try this ☞ **All the words you know**

This is something the children could think about when they are lying in bed waiting to go to sleep. The game is to think of all the colours you know in English, or all the foods, or all the colours. Alternatively, the player can see if they can think of an English word for each letter of the alphabet, seeing how far they can get before getting stuck. For example, *at, bus, come, down, eat, food*. They don't have to start at 'A', they can start later in the alphabet if they want to.

Try this ☞ **Favourite words**

Children could just say their favourite English words and phrases to themselves before they fall asleep.

For older/younger children

The strategy of 'talking in your head' should work for all ages. The older the child, the longer the piece of English they can remember to 'say' in their heads.

Why this works

Echoing new language is a useful technique for creating mental patterns. We know that children need to hear new words many times before they remember them. Saying things in their heads helps speaking, because the brain practises forming the sounds even when the words are kept silent. When children are preparing to speak, this kind of mental preparation will help them sound more fluent.

Children talk to themselves as they play and when they are in bed. This private speech is probably important for language development. Of course, private speech is usually in first language but we may be able to encourage children to use English sometimes too. Using English when playing quietly or just before falling asleep will reinforce the sounds and forms of the language, and will also be quietly pleasurable, adding to the positive feelings that children have about the language. The idea is that this activity will be stress-free and relaxing. It is not about drilling and learning by heart, but about playing with English.

20 Teach long words

Children don't need to be restricted to short words just because they themselves are small. Even very young children enjoy playing with the sounds of long words and have no trouble remembering them.

There are lots of long words that are relevant to the topics in the young learner classroom. Here are just some of them:

- caterpillar
- hippopotamus
- crocodile
- tyrannosaurus rex
- ambulance
- hospital
- automobile
- supermarket
- telephone

Try this ☞ **Make words from a long word**

Once you have introduced your learners to a long word, explore it with them. Together you can make short words from the letters of a long word: first of all any words which you can read in the word, such as *cat*, and *pill* from *caterpillar*. Then you can find other words using the letters of the long word, such as *pat*, *late*, *lip*, *pet*, *tap*, etc. Perhaps you can set your young learners a challenge to see who can find the most words in five minutes.

Try this ☞ **Collecting long words**

Ask the children to tell you long words that they find. Write the words on long strips of paper and count the number of letters together. Put the written words on the wall, organized with the longest at the top. Remind the children to look out for long words at the weekends when they play on their computers or go shopping, and to bring them to class to share.

Teach long words

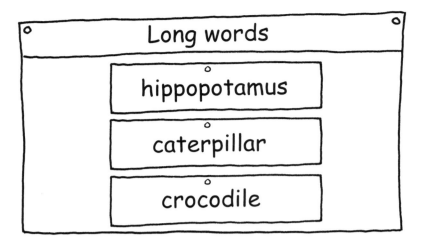

Long words

hippopotamus

caterpillar

crocodile

Try this 👉 **Play games with long words**

Make up a story together that uses as many of the long words as possible.
The caterpillar was going to the supermarket, when the crocodile bumped into him. Oh dear! He broke his leg. The crocodile telephoned for an ambulance. The ambulance came and took him to the caterpillar hospital.

For older/younger children

Keep work on long words oral with very young children. For children learning to read in English, long words can help reading by giving children practise in breaking words into syllables.

Why this works

There is no reason why young children can't work with long words. They enjoy them, and playing with long words in English will build confidence and vocabulary. An interesting phenomenon has been observed with very young children – they may confuse the concept with the word; for example, if you ask for a long word, they may offer 'train'. The word is not long, but the thing itself is long.

Long words often contain short words or syllables that are found in many other words for example, *cat* and *-er* in *caterpillar*. So playing with long words, even if they are not very common words, will give useful practice with vocabulary, and help fluency.

Noticing and playing with the syllables of written words will also help build phonemic awareness and reading skills.

Part 7

Bringing the real world into the classroom

21   English through other subjects

Children love to learn something new about their world. Even though their world may not stretch far beyond their daily lives, there are things to explore that will engage their attention. Learning a language is enhanced when teachers bring the child's world into language lessons because children are eager to know about their world.

Activities where children revise or develop concepts from their other lessons (for example from geography and science) are often called content-based activities. Over time, different activities on the same topic help to reinforce both the language and the concepts. For example, natural science content-based activities might include a chart listing the features of selected animals; a report about what the animals eat; and reading a story about an animal.

↓ SCIENCE AND THE NATURAL WORLD

Children love to see and touch and play with new objects, and they love to think new ideas. When English is used in new and meaningful ways in the classroom, this continually makes English new and exciting. New language is learned best when children do new interesting things and when new ideas are talked about.

Try this ☞ **Comparing objects**

When your learners are learning comparatives in English, they can practise this grammar by making comparisons between things as they would in science lessons. These could be comparisons between objects they have brought into the classroom, such as leaves from the playground, or objects in the classroom that they use for their other lessons. Here are some examples:

- Collect and compare different leaves from the playground (or different shapes in the classroom) and talk about differences, e.g. *shiny/dull; rough/smooth*.
- Compare heavy and light boxes. First estimate together which is heavier, then check on a set of scales.
- Fill different-shaped glasses or bottles with water. Guess which container holds more, then check.

Differences can be written up in graphs and charts.

> Teacher: *Which bottle holds more water, the tall thin one or the short fat one?*
>
> Child: *The tall thin one?*

Teacher: *Let's see. Salma, take the tall thin bottle and fill it with water . . .*
that's it. Now empty the tall thin bottle into the measuring jug.
How many millilitres does the tall thin bottle hold, everyone?

Child: *A hundred.*

Teacher: *That's right, 100 millilitres. Now let's try with the short fat bottle...*

Try this 👉 **Experimenting with magnetism**

Once your young learners have learned about magnetism in their science
lessons, you can revise the concepts in English. You can do most of the talking
but let the children watch and listen, then play and talk about it. You will need
magnets and a range of metal items. Show how a magnet sticks to some of
the items but not to others, or how a spoon can be magnetized by rubbing it
several times in one direction with a magnet.

Teacher: *Watch carefully and tell me what you see.*

Teacher: *The spoon sticks to the magnet. The cup doesn't stick. Why did*
that happen?

Teacher: *Look. The spoon is now a magnet. It can pick up the clip.*

Try this 👉 **Things from nature**

Choose some children from the class to collect items from the classroom that
fit a particular category. For example, if they are collecting 'Things from Nature',
the challenge could be:

● Find something that is alive.
● Find something that is made from a tree.
● Find something that comes from an animal.

View a nature video or look at a nature magazine and ask children to remember
or note down things they see that fit a category, for example, *Remember all the*
red things you see.

You can also do activities in your English lesson that will link with your learners' geography lessons and growing knowledge about the world around them.

Try this ☞ **Photos of places in town**

If you have a digital camera you can take photos of recognizable places in town such as the main square, the supermarket, the main playground, for use in class. Perhaps if you have a classroom character such as a puppet, you can get a friend to help you take photos of the puppet in these places. If you use these pictures to talk about places in town, they will be recognizable and real to your learners.

Try this ☞ **Postcards from around the country/the world**

You can bring in postcards that you have received – or take the opportunity to send one to your class when you are on holiday – for use in class, to make topic work about mountains, lakes, the sea, etc., more immediate. Postcards from different countries can be used to make comparisons between different places in the world (for example climate and lifestyle).

Try this ☞ **Learning about other countries**

English is spoken around the world, so any foreign country can be used as the starting point for activities in the language classroom:

- Ask the children where they would like to go on holiday or to live for a year, and why.
- Collect a list of countries on the board – in first language (we use French as an example here) and in English:

  L'Allemagne   Germany
  Le Kenya   Kenya
  L'Espagne   Spain
  Le Maroc   Morocco

- Choose the most popular country from the list. Talk about the languages used in this country and who might use English, for example, business people, pop singers, tourists. See if you can find pictures and information in English about the country from websites, to build a display, a class website, or a book.

Role-play conversations between people in the pictures (see chapter 25, page 90)

For older children

Older learners can handle more complex topics, and can be expected to contribute more in content-based learning activities. Older learners still need a lot of scaffolding from the teacher, especially in relation to the English they need, but also possibly in relation to the topic knowledge.

Why this works

Children's minds are (or should be if all is well) full of delight and wonder about things around them. Children thrive on intellectual challenge, and so their learning should never become boring and routine. Teachers and parents know that it doesn't take much to stimulate interest in young learners: new activities and games, and new things to look at all do this.

Content-based activities can motivate children to engage in English for a purpose. By listening, speaking, reading, and writing in English to learn something new, children begin to understand that English is not just 'something' to learn, but a way to communicate and make meaning. The materials and activities will support the learners' understanding of the English used to talk about what is happening. The learners' general knowledge of the world will support their understanding of English. Learning new information through English provides opportunities for practising language that is already learned and extending it.

22 English in the world around us

In the school context with its examinations and goals, it can be easy to lose sight of the reasons why English is a useful subject to learn. By showing your young learners that English is used in lots of different contexts outside the classroom, you can help them see the purpose of learning English.

↓ FINDING EXAMPLES OF ENGLISH IN EVERYDAY LIFE

Even young learners will be come into contact with the English language outside school. At home they may see English on TV or on the family computer, and on product packaging labels. In town, they are likely to see English on advertisement posters and billboards. Bringing their attention to the use of English in the world around them will make their English lessons seem more relevant.

Try this ☞ English label cards

Set your learners the task of bringing to class an example of English they have found on a product, such as on a cereal box, or a clothing label, or instructions that came with an electronic gadget. The English can be anything from two words to a whole sentence. Once you have some examples collected by the learners, you can ask them to write down or stick the example on a card, and on another card to write down where they found it. The class can then guess where each example came from and match the cards.

Try this ☞ English signs bingo

Ask the learners to look out for English on signs around town: on advertising billboards, in shop windows, on menus, etc., and to tell you about these over the next week. You can keep a record of the sign, or they can draw it for you, and where they saw it, and then when there are enough (perhaps a minimum of 10), you can go through these together and count up the different places where English is found around your town. Drawings or photographs of the signs can be used to play bingo.

Try this ☞ English in films

As part of a project on cinema, ask the children to list their three favourite films. Ask them which of these films were originally in English. Do a survey to find the class's most popular film, and then organize to watch a short extract from the film in class in English. You can stop the film halfway through to ask the learners who know the film what is going to happen, and if they know any words in English that they will hear.

English speakers in your locality offer opportunities to use English for real purposes. They may be native speakers of English or people who are fluent in English because they use it in their work or social lives. If you can invite them to meet your class, this could create real purpose for your young learners to use English. It will be very motivating for the children to see you talking with a visitor in English or to try out their own English and be understood. Visitors are likely to have a different accent from the teacher, and it is good for the children to hear this and to work at making sense of it.

Try this ☞ **Arrange a visit from an English speaker**

If your school policy permits visitors to a classroom, see if you can find some people locally who are English speakers and who might be suitable to come in to the school. These could be:

- students taking a year out to travel around the world
- older people who have retired to your area
- people in jobs that require them to use English, for example, travel agents or business people
- teachers or others who have studied overseas
- official visitors to your town or city.

Once you have found some reliable people who speak English, you could see about getting permission from your school for them to visit your class. Start with a short visit that is carefully planned. The visitor could be invited to show some pictures of places or people and talk about them.

It is best to prepare the visitor by explaining to them before they come that the children's English is limited and they should speak simply and slowly. Give them in advance a list of words that the children know. Encourage the children to try to work out what the visitor is saying rather than translating everything they say.

Get the children involved: they can write an invitation, prepare questions to ask the visitor, and follow up the visit with a thank-you letter.

Teacher: *Class, this is Heather. Say good morning to Heather!*
Children: *Good morning, Heather.*
Teacher: *Welcome to our school. Do you have some pictures of your house in Scotland to show the children?*
Teacher: *Children, do you want to ask Heather a question?*

✓ *Getting it right*

Planning a visit from an English speaker to your class

Having a visitor come to your class requires forward planning.

- Check your school's policy on having visitors and make sure you comply with it; it may involve running checks on the visitor in advance, letters of permission, or other precautionary measures.
- For the security of everyone involved, never leave the visitor alone with the children.
- Remember that as the teacher you are in charge of the visit. Tell the visitor in advance what you would like them to do.

English in the world around us

Try this ☞ **Make links to establish visits on a regular basis**

If the first visit is a success, you could consider inviting the person to come in at regular intervals. For example, older people who have retired from the UK may be very happy to come in every week or month to talk with, or read to, small groups of children. The children can write to or email visitors when they have returned home to practise more real English.

↓ VARIETIES OF ENGLISH

Because English is spoken in so many countries, there are many different varieties of English, and within these, many different accents. A good way of helping young learners to understand that not all speakers of English have the same accent is to expose them to regional varieties. If you do this in small amounts, this can lead in to discussions of where in the world English is spoken, and show why English is so useful.

Try this ☞ **Listening to regional varieties of English on news broadcasts**

News websites such as the BBC provide short audio and video downloads which you could use with your young learners. A news story from the UK may include interviews with people speaking local dialects of English, whereas the newscaster will speak standard British English. You might also find examples of people speaking different varieties of English, such as Nigerian English, Indian English, or Singapore English. You can usually find suitable content in the 'Science', 'Environment', and sometimes 'Technology' sections of online news services. Make sure you check the whole news item is suitable before using it in class.

Why this works

If we make English relevant to our young learners, this will help them to see why they are learning English and that it will be useful to them. Noticing English as part of the world around them and bringing examples to class and talking about them will help your learners make the link between the real world and the classroom. English-speaking visitors provide real-life examples of English in use, and can answer the learners' curiosity about the language and culture of some English speakers. Listening to regional accents on the news illustrates that although English comes in many different varieties, it can be understood. Your learners may also see how English is often used as a second language by many other people like themselves.

23 Using technology

The world of English texts has expanded from books, newspapers, magazines, and tapes to CDs, DVDs, podcasts, and computer programmes. All texts in English can become a resource for teaching language in the hands of an imaginative teacher. Ultimately, though, it is the meaning within the text rather than the medium (whether it is a book or a digital format) that is the most important for learning.

↓ COMPUTER ACTIVITIES: OFFLINE

Working online (connected to the internet) with young learners has implications for security, but here are some computer-based activities you can use with your young learners without being connected to the internet.

Try this ☞ **Downloading EFL material for children**

There is a lot of free educational material for young learners of English available on the internet (see Useful websites, page 85). Several of these educational websites provide short audio clips of listening material which you could download for use in class, or games which you can use offline.

> Teacher: *What happened to . . .?*
> Teacher: *Take it in turns! Whose turn is it?*
> Child: *It's my turn now.*
> Teacher: *You have to drag-and-drop.*
> Teacher: *You have to colour in.*
> Teacher: *Listen to the computer's instructions.*

Try this ☞ **Jigsaw storytelling with DVD clips**

Divide a video story into two parts. Half the class watch the first part of the story, and the other half watch the second part of the story. Those who watched the first part prepare some questions about what happened in the second part of the story, and vice versa. Then pair up the children from the two groups, and they ask and answer questions to find out the whole story. After a set time, the children will be ready to watch the whole video together – paying extra attention to the part they have heard about but not seen.

Try this ☞ **Computer word processing in English**

Some writing activities can be done on the computer. Using a computer can make young learners' work look very good, especially if an image is inserted into the document to illustrate the work. Electronic files of work can easily be attached to emails to be sent to parents, put on a class blog, or into an electronic portfolio. Other advantages are that the children learn some keyboard skills, they learn to help each other, and they learn some skills of cooperation by taking turns at the keyboard. Using the computer can help children who have difficulties with spelling or handwriting to produce pieces of work that they can be proud of.

Word processing English for special events can be motivating for learners – they can prepare final drafts of stories for others to read, leaflets, programmes for concerts, letters, a class newsletter, and invitations.

↓ COMPUTER ACTIVITIES: ONLINE

There are a lot of educational resources available on the internet designed for use in class, and the internet is such a part of everyday life that it is likely that young learners will already know a lot about how to use it. All schools with internet facilities should have an internet use policy with sections that have to be read and signed by the teacher, the parents, and the young learners. Your learners must understand that they are responsible for their usage of the internet. Before proceeding with activities which use the internet, it is important that your young learners understand that they must only go to the websites that you have given them.

Try this ☞ **Using the internet for topic information ***

As preparation for class, use a search engine to find child-friendly websites about topics in the coursebook. You can either direct the children to these websites in class or download short texts and images from the websites onto a class website for the children to use. You can also save or print out images and texts to use for other activities.

Try this ☞ **Email penfriends**

Email is perfect for writing to penfriends in English (for setting up school email exchanges, see Useful websites, page 105). Scanned-in pictures and other documents can be sent as attachments. If you have the technology, you can also talk to each other on free telephone services and see each other on webcams.

For older children

With older learners there are lots of options using the internet for activities and projects which involve written language.

Try this ☞ **Set up a class blog**

Your older learners can help in setting up a class blog* in two languages – the home language and English. The children can help in planning what should be posted, and in writing the English version (not translating word by word, but carrying the same information in English). They can be encouraged to write a simple post once a week about events in their life.

Try this ☞   **Beat the translator**

Send to your learners an electronic version of a text in English that they can read easily and with pleasure. When they have read it several times in pairs, direct them to an online automatic translator, which they then use to translate the text into their first language. The online translation tool will produce a version which is likely to be inaccurate or odd in some ways. Using this version – and their memory of the text as you sent it – the learners have to reconstruct the original English text. This activity will help your learners see that each language has its expressions and idioms, and that you can't translate word for word. It will also help with accuracy.

Why this works

Most children find computers exciting, and the quality of pictures and sound available through recent technologies is a wonderful improvement that should help the learning of English. As more and more information is available on mobile phones, laptops, and MP3 players, so English learning can be personalized and made really useful for individuals.

Young learners will know from their experiences with English and technology, that the English they hear and see in the media conveys something meaningful to many people. Electronic media therefore offer an excellent resource for reminding children of the meaningfulness of English (as well as giving them opportunities for practice and use). But technology will not make learning happen by itself. You have an important role in selecting and filtering the most valuable reading and visual texts that are interesting, understandable, and provide learning opportunities. You then need to choose or design learning activities to go with the material. Useful videos, DVDs, and computer texts will have plenty of visual support and repetition, and give learners a chance to practise language patterns and learn new vocabulary. Educationally useful games are those that need some understanding or use of English to be played, or those that keep teaching new language.

While you need to find materials which develop the topics and vocabulary of your coursebook, a certain amount of random exposure to English is valuable because it gives children a chance to see how English is being used around the world. However, you need to control the level of language so that the material does not go 'over the children's heads' which would result in them giving up and losing interest.

* Note: The usual precautions should be taken to protect children when using the internet: check your school's internet policy before leading internet activities with your young learners. Parental permissions should be sought as appropriate. Copyright on documents and images should of course be respected.

Part 8

Using make-believe, performance, and metaphor

24 Make-believe

Most young children have lively imaginations. When they play with other children, they pretend to be super-heroes, adults, or imaginary creatures. When they play alone, they create imaginary friends and families, situations, and worlds. Children's imagination can be used to help them learn English.

You can try building up a collection of detailed, colourful pictures of people the children can pretend to be – astronauts, doctors, pop stars, road builders, sailors, historical figures, story characters, etc.

This set of pictures then becomes the basis for many different activities, as listed below. The children can help by bringing in pictures from home, or drawing pictures. Start by making sure that the children know the names of the different people. Of course, these people are going to use English.

Try this ☞ **Being Batman**

Let children choose the picture of who they would like to be. To help them get into role, each child holds their picture. Then you talk to them as if they were that person. Use any English phrases that the children know, such as greetings, to start a conversation.

This activity works well if you model a conversation first by talking to one of the pictures, to show the children that you are pretending that the character in the picture is real. Then try talking with the children and see if they can continue the conversation. Children can also talk to each other in pairs.

Teacher: *Andrew, who are you?*
Andrew: *I'm Batman.*
Teacher: *How are you today, Batman?*
Andrew: *I am very tired.*
Teacher: *Why?*
Andrew: *I saved three children from the sea.*
Teacher: *What are you going to do now?*
Andrew: *I'm going to fly . . . to Singapore!*

Try this ☞ **Pretend play in groups**

Divide the class into groups of four or five in preparation for this activity. Let one child choose a picture to 'be'. They will pretend to be that person, role-playing with other children in the group. For example, a child gets a picture of a gardener or farmer. The other children in the group choose who to pretend to be: the gardener or farmer's children; a naughty child in the garden; or even the crops growing on the farm. Translate the words or phrases that the children want to use into English. Let the children make 'props' for the imaginary scenario and talk as if they were those people.

See what stories they invent – perhaps they are worth writing down?

Try this 👉 **Video-recording pretend play**

Video offers a new set of language-using opportunities:

- Children can watch themselves in role and comment on what they did.
- The teacher can talk about what they see in the video, using more complex language.
- The children can prepare a 'voice over' commentary for the video, practise saying it as the video plays, and record it. The recording and video can then be sent out to parents via email if you have the opportunity.

For older children

Older or more advanced learners can practise more complicated language and ideas, such as *if* sentences: for example, *If I was the farmer, I would chase the naughty children away with my dog.*

Why this works

Psychologists have suggested that pretending allows children to see what it might be like to be an adult for a short time. The pretending can help prepare them for the next stages in their lives. By imagining she is a doctor, a child can try out looking after other people, being powerful and knowledgeable, and having responsibility for 'patients'. By imagining he is a teacher, a child can change roles, take control over his life for a short time, and tell other children what to do. If you watch the children when they play by themselves, you will see the kinds of people they pretend to be, and you can use this as a starting point.

25   Perform it

↓ MAKING AND USING PUPPETS

Puppets are a wonderful aid in the young learner classroom because they add an element of play-acting which can give young learners more freedom to experiment and make mistakes. Sometimes children will talk to a puppet when they are too shy to talk to an adult.

Try this ☞ **Making simple puppets to use in English activities**

The simplest puppet is made by drawing a face on your finger! A cut-out figure or a bag with a face drawn on it can be stuck on to a ruler or stick, or you can make simple finger puppets for use in class. If it is culturally appropriate where you are teaching, you could make sock puppets with the children for them to use in class from time to time.

Try this ☞ **Using finger puppets to rehearse role-play dialogues from the coursebook**

This is a simple but nice way to get the children interested in the dialogues they have learned their coursebooks. A simple 'meeting people' dialogue is perfect for this activity, as the children can work in pairs on the dialogues with their puppets. Let the children practise their dialogues using their puppets, and then ask them to perform in front of the class or in small groups.

Try this ☞ **Use a puppet to give simple instructions for children to act out**

Many topics in the curriculum are easiest to explain and practise by acting out the vocabulary: animals, sports, and everyday activities, for example. Using a puppet to give instructions will make a change in routine and encourage careful listening. For example, instructions for everyday activities could be:

- *Wash your face.*
- *Brush your teeth.*
- *Get dressed.*
- *Put your coat on.*

When your learners have become familiar with simple instructions, you can give more complicated instructions:

- *Clean your shoes, then put your coat on.*
- *When you have finished brushing your teeth, dry your face.*

↓ ROLE-PLAY AND SIMPLE DRAMA ACTIVITIES

Role-play and simple drama activities can help children to practise English and to experiment with language they have learned. Role-play and drama can either be rehearsed, when children first prepare or write down and learn what they are going to say, or they can be spontaneous, when children create their own language as they take part in the mini-drama. Performing can be fun and can help children to relate the language to their own experiences.

Try this ☞ **Extending dialogues from the coursebook**

Give the class a dialogue that they know from their coursebook, and divide the class into small groups. They then work in their groups to extend the dialogue (with some teacher help), adding different ideas, or making it funny. When they are ready, they can perform their version for the class (see Table 25.1).

Coursebook dialogue	Children's funny dialogue
Speaker 1: What's your favourite colour? Speaker 2: It's blue. What's yours? Speaker 1: It's red.	Speaker 1: What's your favourite colour? Speaker 2: I don't like colours. I like black. What about you? Speaker 1: I don't like colours either. I like white!
Speaker 1: What's your favourite sport? Speaker 2:. It's cycling. What's yours? Speaker 1: It's skating.	Speaker 1: What's your favourite sport? Speaker 2: It's catching monkeys. Do you like catching monkeys? Speaker 1: No. It's cruel.

TABLE 25.1   *Extending coursebook dialogues*

Try this ☞ **Open pair dialogues**

One child in each pair is given the phrases of a dialogue. The other child has to answer and respond as spontaneously as they can.

Try this ☞ **Talking on the phone**

Let children talk to each other using old or toy telephones to stimulate a rehearsed or simultaneous dialogue. You can teach the children phrases to help them keep talking:

Perform it

- *Hello?*
- *Hello. Is that Elena?*
- *Pardon?*
- *Sorry, what did you say?*
- *Can you repeat that?*
- *Do you agree?*
- *I'm not sure.*
- *I think . . .*
- *I'm sorry, I don't know.*
- *I have to go now. Goodbye!*
- *See you later, bye!*

For older/younger children

Younger children can mime or act out a well known story as the teacher reads it aloud. Older children can listen to a story, note the main points of the story with the teacher, and then improvise the story in pairs or in group work. Older children can also perform and learn a scripted play. They may be given the script, or can write the script with the help of the teacher.

Why this works

Children naturally engage in drama in their first language to help them develop their understanding of themselves, of others, and of the world. This kind of play helps to extend their first language. Similarly in English, they have an opportunity to understand their world and extend their language through drama. Drama activities in English are unlikely to just happen in the play corner (unless children are immersed in the foreign language as in a bilingual programme). Teachers need to plan for role-playing and drama, firstly by organizing fully-rehearsed role-plays and mimes in which children act out a memorized part prepared beforehand; and secondly enabling children to take part in more open dialogues, for example by talking to a puppet held by the teacher or a friend.

Using a foreign language can feel like performing anyway because the language is artificial and new. It doesn't yet 'fit' the user in the same way that a language learned from birth does. By using performance in class, you can use the 'foreignness' of language-learning to your advantage. Pretending and performing can release children to feel freer in the language.

26

Use metaphor

Everyone can use metaphor. Metaphors (and some similes) often compare two things that are very different:

The moon is a balloon.

Sometimes they talk about one thing as if it were something different:

I am so happy I feel as if I could fly!

We use metaphors in poems to express feelings but ordinary language is also full of metaphor in the form of idiomatic words and phrases:

Could you give me a hand with this heavy bag? (meaning please help me…)

What a lovely warm smile!

While it can be difficult to learn idioms because they are often quite odd grammatically, this chapter shows how simple metaphors can be understood and constructed by the children using the grammar and vocabulary found in early coursebooks and curricula.

Try this ☞ Explore simple idioms which are part of classroom language

You can introduce your learners to the idea of metaphor by exploring some of the metaphors that they already use or hear in their own language, and then exploring some of those that you sometimes use in the classroom:

- *Keep an eye on the time please* (= Regularly check what time it is to be sure we aren't late)
- *Give me a hand with the books please* (= Help me)
- *It's boiling in this room today* (= It's very hot)
- *I hope you don't catch a cold* (= Become ill with a cold)
- *You have worked so hard – you deserve a medal!* (= I am very pleased with you).

Children often enjoy exploring the literal meaning of metaphors, and doing this activity makes metaphors seem less strange.

Try this ☞ Making metaphor associations

This activity stimulates your learners' imagination and helps make the language used memorable.

Give the class an example, and then encourage them to give you their associations. This could be in their first language if they don't know the word in English. If the ideas are in your learners' first language, see if they can help you translate. If you write the children's suggestions in English on the board, you – or they – can draw a picture of the ideas to help them remember the suggestions in English.

Teacher: *What things are warm? What things feel like 'warm'?*

Teacher: *What do you think of when you hear the word 'strong'?*

Teacher: *What things are 'golden'?*

Teacher: *What things feel like 'happiness'?*

Some associations that the children might make are listed in Table 26.1.

Warm	Strong	Golden	Happiness
– a hug from my mother	– bright red	– sunshine	– birds singing
– when I get my sums right	– a loud noise on the drum	– a lion	– balloons
– a blanket	– feeling very happy or very frightened	– field of corn	– bubbles
– sunshine	– a picture drawn with thick lines	– sunset	– parties
– a happy day like my birthday	– an elephant	– my grandmother's smile	
– laughing	– a big tree		
	– thunder		
	– a warrior		
	– steel		

TABLE 26.1   *Adjectives and some possible associations*

Other adjectives we can use metaphorically include: loud, cold, soft, hard, full, empty, bright, and dark.

Try this ☞ **Describing people with metaphors**

Once they have the idea of using metaphor, you can ask your learners to use metaphors to describe themselves or imaginary people:

I am a warm friend to Anwar. I can run like the wind. My hair is golden and my eyes are brown like honey.

I am brave like a lion and strong as steel. I can fly like a bird. Who am I? (Superman)

↓ PROJECT AND GROUP WORK

Class work on metaphor is a good opportunity for group work, as the more people there are, the more ideas there are to work with. Below are two ideas for group work, the first developing metaphors for the weather, and the second working on the symbolism of colours.

Try this ☞ **Make a collective poem from weather metaphors**

Firstly, revise the vocabulary for the weather with your class. Then your learners can work individually or in pairs to make a sentence describing a weather condition by using an image. For example, a sentence about strong wind could be:

The wind blows like an angry horse.

If you have a large class, you could put the pairs or individuals into groups and allocate different types of weather, for example, a hot day in the summer when it starts to rain; a rainy day in spring; a cold, icy night in the winter; or a snowstorm which clears up and leaves everything covered in snow.

You may need to help the learners with their sentences if they are not used to this kind of activity. When they have finished, collect the sentences and read them to the class, saying the sentence as dramatically as possible. Together with the class, create a poem from the sentences by deciding the order in which the sentences sound best. Together, decide on a last line that sounds different from the others. Here is an example of a collective weather poem describing a storm:

The wind blows like an angry horse.
The rain falls like little hammers on the roof.
The thunder roars like a dragon.
And the lightning cracks.
I feel very small and scared.

Try this ☞ **Exploring how different cultures use colours**

This will help develop your learners' intercultural competence and is a good group project activity. As a whole group, explore the symbolic meanings for a colour, first of all in the culture(s) of the learners you are teaching, and then in other cultures. For example:

- Red is used internationally to signal danger. It is the colour of blood. It is also the colour of a heart, and is the colour of love. Red is used at Christmas, it is a colour of celebration. In China, red means good luck, and people wear red when they get married.
- White in India carries the idea of sadness and is worn at funerals but in Europe it carries the idea of purity and is worn at weddings.
- Green is about the natural world and the environment. Green is the colour of spring and being young. It is also the colour of jealousy.

Divide your class into small groups and help them collect information and pictures (using the internet or information you have found) from different cultures that show how colours are used. As a group, they can then make posters about their colour, and then when they have finished they can present their posters to the rest of the class.

Why this works

Metaphor is not difficult for children. Many words that children learn early on can be used to make metaphors, creating strong and colourful images with the new language. Children will be able to understand what is meant, even if they don't understand everything that is said.

Metaphor can make English come alive for the children. Instead of learning only concrete vocabulary, they have the opportunity to play with words and create exciting ideas.

Part 9

For the teacher: language and cultural contexts

27 Keep developing your own English

This unit is addressed to teachers who use English as a foreign or second language themselves.

As a teacher of young children, you will be teaching simple English and you may find that this is not challenging enough for you after a while. Finding ways of keeping your own English active and growing will keep you inspired and will inspire the children you teach. Your young learners need you to be fluent and confident, and to enjoy using English.

↓ OUTSIDE THE CLASSROOM

We all know that we can improve our foreign language skills by studying but it is hard to find the time, and sometimes to find the motivation. Listening and reading activities in English do not have to be from a textbook, alone at your desk – there are all sorts of materials in English for people interested in getting more exposure to the language.

Try this ☞ Reading magazines in English

When you pass through an airport, you could buy several magazines in English on topics that interest you to read over the coming months. These could be celebrities, photography, or decorating – the actual content doesn't matter; what matters is that you will be motivated to read sections of the magazines in your free time.

You could introduce a magazine box to the staff room where you can leave your magazines when you have finished with them. They can either be a reading resource for other teachers or a source of pictures for their young learners to use.

Try this ☞ Reading children's books

There are many well-written and beautifully illustrated books written for English-speaking children that adults can enjoy too. The advantage of reading books like these is that they are easy to read and so can be fitted into a busy schedule.

You could also try reading novels written for teenagers or unsimplified versions of familiar fairy stories and folk tales.

Audio recordings of books, or podcasts of books that you download onto an MP3 player, are another option: they are excellent for building and maintaining language skills (see Useful websites, page 105).

Try this ☞ **Use the internet as a source of free material**

There is a lot of information available on the internet for free, from educational resources for all levels of ability, to songs in English, and English-speaking radio stations. It is worth spending some time finding resources that you find interesting and trying to make a regular time to dedicate to improving your English using internet resources.

Try this ☞ **Using Web 2.0 in English**

With the development of internet technology, a feature of modern internet is Web 2.0, which is where the content on the website is uploaded by the users of the site. These are typically social networks, wikis, and blogs. Some Web 2.0 sites are used by teachers who wish to share their resources. These can be a wonderful source of ideas and inspiration, and they are in English. If you prefer, you can start by reading Web 2.0 materials, and then add to them when you are ready. All wikis, blogs, and social networks have privacy settings so that you choose how public you want your postings to be.

Try this ☞ **Travelling with English**

A good way of preparing for your English lessons is to rehearse the language you will need. You can do this on your way to work: if you drive to work, say out loud the language that you will use in the lesson. If you use public transport, say it silently 'in your head'! A journey also offers time to listen to CDs or podcasts in English too.

Try this ☞ **Talking to other English teachers in English**

You don't have to talk to native-speakers to practise English. Perhaps you could get together a small group of teachers who want to practise English and eat a meal together once a month, speaking English. You could watch an English film at the cinema or on DVD and then talk about it, or you could share teaching ideas, reporting on a problem in your class, a lesson that went well, or a young learner who made a breakthrough.

↓ IN THE CLASSROOM

If English is not your first language, you may feel slightly unsure about using it in the classroom. But there is more to language than words: gesture, tone of voice, and demonstration all help to show meaning, and they can work for you in the classroom. Translation is a last resort, but is an area in which you are expert.

Try this ☞ **Speak confidently to the children**

If you show yourself to be confident when speaking English, your young learners will believe that you can speak English really well. This will have the benefit of increasing your confidence as well as helping your learners see that speaking English is an attainable goal.

Try this ☞ **Interact with the children in English**

You can show that you expect your learners to be able to understand English by using English in interactions with them. Instructions, for example, are used again and again, and so if you can give them in English, the children will learn by doing and then really know this language. Other areas of interaction in English are your responses to the children's questions and comments, and when you praise the children's work or behaviour. They will be able to tell by your tone of voice and your expression that you are pleased with them, and will be encouraged to try to understand what you are saying.

 *Getting it right*

Knowing when to use your learners' first language

Giving instructions, answering questions, and giving praise in English are all good, but if the children are looking unsure, check that they have understood. Clarify the English by using mime, demonstration, or translation (perhaps by a child who has understood). Once the meaning is clear, repeat in English several times to give them the opportunity to learn the new words and phrases.

Teacher: *Good morning, everyone.*

Teacher: *Now, sit down and open your books at page three.*

Teacher: *Be quiet now.*

Teacher: *Does everyone have a pencil/pen?*

Teacher: *Well done!*

Teacher: *You are very good today.*

Why this works

The best way to improve your English is to use it, if possible in real communication with others who can speak English. This way, you activate what you know about English grammar and vocabulary.

You will improve your English by taking risks. Be ready to make mistakes when you talk with other teachers or friends. Ask them to point out if you make a mistake – but not every time you make a mistake – just perhaps at the end of your discussion. And then have a good laugh about it.

Young children are excellent at learning accents and pronunciation. Make yourself a great model for them to copy.

28 Learning a new cultural context

This chapter is addressed to teachers for whom English is a first language and who find themselves teaching English in a new cultural context.

You are a source of the English language and need to make effective use of your language knowledge so that your learners develop. To do that, you need to be sensitive to the context that your learners come from, and that you are living in.

↓ OUTSIDE SCHOOL

The first way of understanding your learners' context is to find ways of immersing yourself in the culture that is local to where you are teaching. This could be on a one-to-one basis, or by getting involved in a local group of some kind. The important thing is to have contact with local people so that you can find out about local culture and perspectives, which will help you understand your learners better.

Try this ☞ **A language exchange with another adult**

Find someone who is willing to teach you the local language in exchange for practising their English. You can meet up (somewhere public, like a café) for an hour, speaking for the first half hour in English and the second half hour in the local language or vice versa. If you are lucky, you will also make a friend who will fill you in on cultural conventions and everyday life: food, celebrations, family life, social relations, etc.

Look for someone your own age, but be open to friendships with older and younger people.

✓ *Getting it right* **Finding a language exchange partner**

It is probably best not to arrange a language learning exchange with a parent of one of the children in your class, since that might worry other parents. Perhaps parents can put you in touch with a prospective language exchange partner instead.

Try this ☞ **Joining a club or group**

Pursuing an interest when you are abroad can be a good way of getting to know people to talk to, as it brings you into contact with people with whom you have something in common. Perhaps you could sing in a choir, or go to dancing lessons, or motor vehicle repair classes – anything that you enjoy that will bring you into contact with local people. If the idea of an evening class does not really appeal, you could join in community activities, like beach cleaning or harvesting.

Try this ☞ **Dealing with prejudices**

Your own: be aware that while you are new and dealing with stressful challenges, deep-seated prejudices and assumptions may rise to the surface. You may not like this about yourself, but it is not an unusual response to stress. To calm your mind, it can help to write down your thoughts (and then destroy the notes).

Other expatriates' prejudices: while it can be a relief to find fellow native speakers, be cautious about linking yourself with people you may later discover have questionable opinions about life in your new context.

Try this ☞ **Finding a local mentor**

Look for a wise colleague who will help you settle in, provide advice, and be willing to answer your questions. Check new ideas with this person before implementing them to make sure they won't offend in the local culture.

↓ AT SCHOOL

As a native speaker of English, teaching English comes with a certain responsibility. As a native speaker, you speak fluently the language that your learners are piecing together bit by bit, and it is important to use your 'expertise' wisely and avoid overloading them with too much of your language. Similarly, non-native speaker teachers of English may find your language expertise intimidating: a helpful and open attitude on your part can help your 'native speaker' status be a benefit for the whole school, not just your class.

Try this ☞ **Grading your language**

Too much talk may confuse learners. It may be tempting to explain the meanings of words, to tell learners about the history of the language, or to suggest different ways of saying the same thing, but don't overwhelm your learners with language.

Your language should be not too simple for the learners and not too difficult for them but 'just right' – which means slightly challenging but comprehensible with some effort.

If you grade your language in this way, and accompany it with gestures, objects, or pictures, the children will be encouraged to pay attention to what you are saying.

Try this ☞ **Monitoring yourself**

If you have the resources to do this, make and watch a video of the children when you are teaching every so often to check your language 'tuning'. You can monitor how well the learners understand what you are saying by looking at their eyes – are the children alert and interested? If not, then you need to grade your language.

Try this ☞   **Being a resource**

Be interested in what your learners want to find out. Offer yourself as a living dictionary ready to give translations (if you can) and explanations when your learners ask you. Offer to work with fellow teachers making materials together or just chatting in English in an informal group.

Why this works

As an incomer to the community, you will stand out and be noticed. As a teacher of young children, you will be scrutinized and welcomed by parents, colleagues, and community leaders. It is rewarding but not easy to learn how to live in a new context; all that you learn will help you better understand your children and how they learn.

Useful websites

News and current affairs

http://news.bbc.co.uk

The BBC news site is a good source of video and audio files and contains some videos suitable for use with learners aged 10–12. The 'Science and environment' section, contains videos such as 'Turtle turns 70'; or 'Giant sea snail on show'.

www.cnn.com

The US site CNN has similar content to the BBC, some of which is suitable for supervised young learners.

Free educational material for young learners

http://www.britishcouncil.org/kids.htm

British Council

http://www.bbc.co.uk/learning/subjects/childrens_learning.shtml

The BBC children's learning section guides you to resources categorized by age groups.

School email exchanges and project partnerships

www.Elanguages.org

www.Globalgateway.org

These websites share information between schools wishing to collaborate on project work or to organize a school email exchange.

Podcasts of children's books in English

http://www.podiobooks.com

This website of free podcasts includes a section of children's books and others.

www.librivox.org

Find here free audio podcasts of published books in the public domain

Social networks

www.ning.com

You can set up your own social network for free using this Web 2.0 site.